"*Perichoresis* is an inexhaustibly attractive idea, invoked in Trinitarian revivals, and essential, some believe, to an understanding of the divine fellowship for which we humans were made. In this wonderfully lucid study of John Damascene, Charles Twombly provides what is most needed to ground contemporary reflection: a discerning account of what perichoresis has historically meant, not only to this 'last of the Fathers' but to the cumulative tradition he bequeathed to Christendom, East and West."

—CAROL ZALESKI
Professor of World Religions, Smith College

"St. John Damascene famously said, 'I shall say nothing of my own,' and much modern scholarship has taken him at his word. Yet, as Charles Twombly shows, John Damascene was a truly original theologian. His notion of *perichoresis*, 'co-inherence,' though it has precedents in earlier Fathers, becomes in his theology a golden thread, drawing together his understanding of the Trinity, the incarnation, and our union with God, our deification. This lucid and profound study makes a major contribution to our understanding of John and his enduring significance."

—ANDREW LOUTH
Professor emeritus of Patristic and Byzantine Studies, Durham University

Perichoresis and Personhood

Princeton Theological Monograph Series
K. C. Hanson, Charles M. Collier, D. Christopher Spinks,
and Robin A. Parry, Series Editors

Recent volumes in the series:

Matthias Grebe
*Election, Atonement, and the Holy Spirit:
Through and Beyond Barth's Theological Interpretation of Scripture*

Brock Bingaman
*All Things New: The Trinitarian Nature of the Human Calling
in Maximus the Confessor and Jürgen Moltmann*

Stephanie Mar Brettmann
*Theories of Justice:
A Dialogue with Karol Wojtyla/John Paul II and Karl Barth*

Alfred H. Yuen
Barth's Theological Ontology of Holy Scripture

Bernadette McNary-Zak
Seeking in Solitude: A Study of Select Forms of Eremitic Life and Practice

Melanie L. Dobson
Health as a Virtue: Thomas Aquinas and the Practice of Habits of Health

Peter Laughlin
Jesus and the Cross: Necessity, Meaning, and Atonement

Andrew Shepherd
The Gift of the Other: Levinas, Derrida, and a Theology of Hospitality

Brendon Thomas Sammon
*The God Who Is Beauty: Beauty as a Divine Name in Thomas Aquinas
and Dionysius the Areopagite*

Perichoresis and **Personhood**
God, Christ, and Salvation in John of Damascus

CHARLES C. TWOMBLY

Foreword by
MYK HABETS

☙PICKWICK *Publications* • Eugene, Oregon

PERICHORESIS AND PERSONHOOD
God, Christ, and Salvation in John of Damascus

Princeton Theological Monograph Series 216

Copyright © 2015 Charles C. Twombly. All rights reserved. Except for brief quotations in critical publications or reviews, no part of this book may be reproduced in any manner without prior written permission from the publisher. Write: Permissions, Wipf and Stock Publishers, 199 W. 8th Ave., Suite 3, Eugene, OR 97401.

Pickwick Publications
An Imprint of Wipf and Stock Publishers
199 W. 8th Ave., Suite 3
Eugene, OR 97401

www.wipfandstock.com

ISBN 13: 978–1-62032–180–5

Cataloging-in-Publication data:

Twombly, Charles C.

    Perichoresis and personhood : god, Christ, and salvation in John of Damascus / Charles C. Twombly ; foreword by Myk Habets.

    Princeton Theological Monograph Series 216

    xvi + 114 p. ; 23 cm. —Includes bibliographical references.

    ISBN 13: 978–1-62032–180–5

    1. John, of Damascus, Saint. 2. Salvation. 3. Trinity. 4. Fathers of the church. I. Habets, Myk. II. Title. III. Series.

BR1720.J59 T86 2015

Manufactured in the U.S.A.

For Sheila, Lee, Ian

When the Lord restored the fortunes of Zion,
we were like those who dream.
Then our mouth was filled with laughter,
and our tongue with shouts of joy;
then they said among the nations,
"The Lord has done great things for them."
The Lord has done great things for us;
we are glad.

Restore our fortunes, O Lord,
like the watercourses in the Negeb!
May those who sow in tears
reap with shouts of joy!
He that goes forth weeping,
bearing the seed for sowing,
shall come home with shouts of joy,
bringing his sheaves with him.

—Psalm 126 (RSV)

Contents

Foreword by Myk Habets ix

Preface xi

Acknowledgments xiii

Abbreviations xv

1 **Introduction** 1

2 ***Perichoresis* and the Trinity** 8
The Scope of Book One
The Inner Logic of John Damascene's Trinitarian Theology

3 ***Perichoresis* and Christ** 47
Chalcedon and After: A Brief Sketch
Perichoresis in John Damascene's Christology

4 ***Perichoresis* and Salvation** 88
Perichoresis or Participation?
Humanity's Original Union with God
The Loss of Union with God through the Fall
Union Regained through Christ's Redemption
Final Union with God in the Life to Come

Epilogue 104

Bibliography 107

Foreword

PERICHORESIS HAS BECOME ONE OF THOSE PLASTIC WORDS BANDIED ABOUT the theosphere with reckless abandon. Originally a term used in the tradition as a way to describe the hypostatic union, it quickly made its way into Trinitarian discourse as an analogy for the unity of the three divine persons in the one being of God. In recent theology the term has been applied to marriage, church, and even creation in ways that stretch the credibility of the term and threaten the ongoing usefulness of the concept. Charles Twombly has done the church a double service in offering one of the few book-length studies of the term and an insightful examination of the way it was used by one of the more important theologians of the Trinity, namely, John of Damascus. This fine study by one with an eye for critical detail and a deft touch deserves a wide reading.

The Syrian monk and priest John of Damascus has long been a favorite of theologians of the Trinity, East and West alike; and yet his theology has not received the direct attention it deserves. As the last of the Eastern Orthodox Fathers, it fell to John Damascene to both gather up the tradition that had been handed on to him and to further enrich it with his not unsubstantial skills as a polymath. His legacy is thus as the major systematizer of Eastern Christian thought up to the eighth century. His *magnum opus*, *Fountain Head of Knowledge*, along with his treatise on the defense of holy images, has cast a long shadow over subsequent sacramentology. In theology it is his magisterial work *On The Orthodox Faith* (the third part of *The Fount of Knowledge*) that has had the most enduring impact. In this work John stands on the shoulders of his predecessors as he attempts to tease out the implications of Chalcedonian Christology and Nicene Trinitarianism.

Throughout *On The Orthodox Faith* John draws upon the theology of Gregory of Nazianzus especially in order to explicate doctrines of God, cosmology, and Christology, drawn around the theme of *theosis*. John narrates what had by this time (d. c. 750) become pretty standard fare in Eastern Orthodox theology, namely, the creation of Adam and Eve in the divine image and likeness, the loss of the likeness in the fall—the tragic *katabasis*—and the work of Christ, who, through the great exchange, once more made it possible for humanity to participate in the divine nature—the great *anabasis*. In this connection John often repeats the axiom of Gregory of Nazianzus, "That which has not been assumed has not been healed." John then explicated the ways in which *theosis* is attained in this life as the believer is incorporated into Christ by water and Spirit, through baptism and Eucharist. By communion we partake of the divinity of Jesus as we proleptically enter into the eschatological reality in the present. In such a way *theosis* forms one of the integrating motifs of John's work, giving sense to the disparate parts.

There are other ways to read John's work, however, and Charles Twombly shows one such alternative account. The concept of *perichoresis* and the Trinity is so pervasive in On The Orthodox Faith that it too is a viable candidate for an integrative motif. Such is Twombly's argument and here for the first time in a published monograph the perichoretic Trinitarianism of John Damascene is laid out for the reader in detail and with clarity. The focus of Twombly's account is the Damascene's work On The Orthodox Faith, and the way in which the concept of *perichoresis* allows him to apply and develop a consistent Chalcedonian theology to his doctrines of God, Christ, and by derivation salvation, and thereby give greater clarity to the Trinity, incarnation, and soteriology. As Twombly argues, "*Perichoresis* in John's thought, functions as a magnet drawing various iron filings together into a coherent pattern."

Although first written as a thesis in 1992, Twombly's account presages that of much recent work on pro-Nicene and Chalcedonian history and the subsequent development of doctrine of the Trinity. Eschewing "two-camp" theories and a "flat" account of doctrinal development, Twombly highlights the tradition inherited by John and the ways in which the Damascene added to and enriched that tradition with his own insights. The account of John's theology in this volume is rich and profound, offering insights into the nature of language, theological method, Trinitarian theology, Christology, and doctrinal uses of philosophy. As such it offers that rare blend of historical-philosophical-biblical-theological scholarship too rarely seen in the academy today. Like his subject matter, Twombly approaches his topic with reverence and considerable skill; all of which is submitted to the act of worship. Like the work of *Chrysorrhoas* himself, Twombly's eloquence is here on display in service to the church.

Myk Habets
Lecturer in Systematic Theology
Carey Baptist College
Auckland, New Zealand

Preface

THIS STUDY ATTEMPTS TO FILL A DOUBLE VOID. APART FROM ANDREW Louth's magisterial work on John of Damascus in 2002, full-scale treatments of this great theologian, hymn writer, polemicist, and pioneer systematizer are conspicuous by their absence, especially in the last fifty years. Given the so-called Trinitarian renaissance in the same time period, the virtual non-existence of extensive work on the theme of *perichoresis* (mutual indwelling, interpenetration) is even more surprising. The term now pops up everywhere, in connection with the Trinity, Christology, and even ecclesiology and social relations; but it rarely receives more than a handful of pages. Perhaps the tide is turning. Emmanuel Durand (of the Institut Catholique de Paris) has now offered us a 2005 study of *perichoresis* (in French) that is extensive in scope and will, we hope, be translated someday.

My study, by contrast with Durand's, is an intensive probing of a single theologian and attempts to lay bare the structure and theological implications of *perichoresis* in the context of writings that have given it its classical shape. As such, what follows aims at a kind of ground-clearing, a patient examination of how the term is actually used in concrete settings and in relation to central Christian dogma. The value of this, for me, is twofold: it can aid constructive theologians to employ the term with greater depth and precision; and it can lay the groundwork for others to build on as they explore *perichoresis* in its Greek and Latin forms throughout the course of theological history. Much more needs to be done, and my hope is that other scholars (especially younger ones) will find my work to be an essential starting point for their own work.

Journeys often begin with maps. Here are some words of guidance before embarking. Chapter 1 sketches John Damascene's background and identifies *perichoresis* as a term used to give intelligibility to relationships in which both identity and difference are crucial. The second chapter explores mutual indwelling in relation to the Trinity and argues that the use of Chalcedonian phrases such as "without confusion" and "without separation" are crucial in John's articulation of three *hypostaseis* ("persons") sharing one *ousia* ("essence" or "substance"). Chapter 3 examines *perichoresis* in connection with the two natures of the incarnate Word. The reciprocal influence of Trinitarian logic is noted: the locus of will and operation/energy in the common nature of the Trinity and not in the individual "persons" is now used as a rationale for asserting the presence of two wills and two operations in Christ. Even though the Logos is the "person" of both natures, each nature possesses its own intrinsic capacities. Mutual indwelling enables the separate natures to work in union. The fourth chapter argues that, in relation to salvation, the language of participation or communion more adequately describes the nature of the relationship involved because the union of human and divine in redemption has an element of inconstancy missing in John's employment of *perichoresis* in terms of God and Christ. The epilogue will provide a brief summary of the previous chapters and encourage further work on the themes of the book.

Acknowledgments

"Others have labored, and we have entered into their labors." A focused interest in *perichoresis* began for me in a seminar on the Trinity offered by Jürgen Moltmann at Emory University in 1983. Professor Moltmann has been a key figure in the so-called Trinitarian renaissance. Even though my thinking moves in a different direction from his, I recollect with great fondness his generosity and humanity and the inspiration his seminar provided. Other "teachers" along the way, official or otherwise, have provided their own inspiration. A list could fill pages, but I would single out a few whose shaping influence has been enormous: Roberta Bondi (my dissertation director at Emory), Don Saliers and Brooks Holifield (also at Emory), David Hubbard and Geoffrey Bromiley (at Fuller Theological Seminary), Bob Gundry (at Westmont College), and Hal Knight (now at St Paul School of Theology), all of whom demonstrated through both their thinking and their living how the life of a Christian scholar should be played out. Others whom I was privileged to encounter briefly and whose writings matter much to me are Thomas F. Torrance (above all), John Zizioulas, John Meyendorff, and Paulos Mar Gregorios. In recent years, I have benefited by another renaissance, that of patristics generally, in which younger scholars are making amazing contributions. I would single out Lewis Ayres, Khaled Anatolios, Michel Barnes, John Behr, and Paul Blowers from a list that could be greatly extended. Andrew Louth, who might be pleased to be grouped with "younger scholars," deserves special mention. His own work on John Damascene is a landmark event.

Others have contributed in their own way. Myk Habets and Mike Gibson both played crucial roles in getting me to offer this work for publication; in some ways, this is their book too. Father Carlton Shuford and his dear wife, Kathy, along with the Bible class at Grace Church in Sandersville, Georgia, offered spiritual support and enthusiasm that made a real difference too.

Those who labor in the fields of scholarship know only too well that, behind their toils, there stands a long-suffering spouse and (often) long-suffering children. Our children, Lee Twombly Olson and Ian Twombly, have played their own roles and share our vision of a life of service. As for my wife, Sheila, more than anyone else, she has given me the love and companionship without which the whole venture that culminates in this book would be not only impossible but without point. She dared to believe that her husband should follow his dream as far as it would take him; her steadfast confidence, born from that shared vision of what our lives should be about, was the ballast that kept the family ship from tipping over on those many occasions when my work pulled me away from matters of pressing concern. Our life together has been my most profound education. Now, I dedicate this book to all three. If love could burst one's heart like a balloon, I'm a goner.

Added Note: I gratefully acknowledge the kind and generous permission granted me by the director of the Catholic University Press of America, Dr. Trevor Lipscombe, to make extensive quotations from Frederic H. Chase Jr.'s translation of the writings of John of Damascus in the CUA series, The Fathers of the Church, whose editor, Dr. Carole Monica Burnett, not only gave super assistance but was a delight to correspond with.

Abbreviations

CD	Karl Barth, *Church Dogmatics*
D.n.	[Pseudo-] Dionysius, *De Divinis Nominibus* [*On the Divine Names*]
Greg N.	Gregory of Nyssa
Greg Naz	Gregory of Nazianzen
Haers.	John of Damascus, *Liber de haerisibus* (Kotter IV)
Joh.D.	John of Damascus/Damascene
MPG	John of Damascus, *Opera*. Patrologia graeca (J.-P. Migne), vols. 94–96
OF	John of Damascus, (*Exact Exposition of*) *The Orthodox Faith/ De Fide Orthodoxa*
Schriften	P. Bonifatius Kotter, *Die Schriften des Johannes von Damaskos*, vols. 1–5

I

Introduction

THIS STUDY ATTEMPTS A CLOSE EXAMINATION OF HOW A KEY THEOLOGIcal term, *perichoresis*, functions in the thought of John of Damascus (c. 675–c. 749). *Perichoresis*, which has variously been rendered in English as "interpenetration," "coinherence," "mutual indwelling," and "mutual immanence," gained classical expression in John's writings, especially his *Exact Exposition of the Orthodox Faith* (*Ekdosis Akribas tas Orthodoxou Pisteos*), frequently referred to by its Latin name, *De Fides Orthodoxa*. Since the eighth century, it has exercised an almost continous influence on both Trinitarian and christological discussion and, in our day, has played a crucial role in the theologies of Karl Barth and Jürgen Moltmann.[1]

Ironically, given both the persistent use of *perichoresis* in doctrinal discussion and the frequent appeal to John of Damascus as a primary source for the word, few scholars have attempted to probe the language of mutual indwelling in terms of its historical usages. More surprising, given John's ongoing importance as a shaper of theological traditions, is the virtual absence of full-scale studies of his particular employment of *perichoresis*.[2]

It might be asked at the outset why the term has persisted. Our concluding chapter will offer a few brief suggestions by way of an answer to that

---

1. Barth's use of *perichoresis* is worked out within the Trinitarian shape of his whole theological project; see, especially, *CD* I/1:425, 431, 454–56. Moltmann's use of the term comes out most clearly in an important section of *The Trinity and the Kingdom*, 174–76. Moltmann sees in the "family" character of the Trinity the basis for a social ethic based on full equality.

2. The reader is referred to the work of G. L. Prestige, Lars Thunberg, August Deneffe, H. A. Wolfson, and Vladimir Lossky as listed in the bibliography. Apart from the essay-length studies of Prestige and Deneffe, these sources consist of brief, but rich, discussions. Excepting the present study, the only book-length study of *perichoresis*, either in some broad historical context or in relation to a single thinker, is Durand's *La perichorese*.

question, but the bulk of the present work has the weightier task of carefully tracking the various ways *perichoresis* works in the overall pattern of the thought of John Damascene to illuminate his understanding of God, Christ, and salvation. All three of these loci, at least in their classical patristic forms, entail notions of mutual indwelling. An exacting study of John's use of *perichoresis* should not only help us gain clarity about the term itself but should aid us in grasping in more penetrating ways his manner of setting forth three crucial doctrines.

But why study John of Damascus? The question does not automatically answer itself since assessments of John have varied widely.[3] Nearly all, however, acknowledge the important role he plays in theological history. His monumental work, *The Fount of Knowledge* (*Paga Gnoseos* or *Fons Scientiae*), of which *The Orthodox Faith* forms the third and most important part, is one of the few efforts at systematization in the Christian East in patristic times. Not only did it establish a model for a kind of scholastic articulation of doctrine, in both the East and the West, but it also summed up the Chalcedonian tradition as it developed in the nearly three centuries after the Fourth Council.

This harvesting of one strand of ancient Christian thought is important for at least three reasons. First of all, it helps to place the earlier christological controversies in truer perspective. It is a common mistake to see the Council of Chalcedon (451 CE) as the end of the debates about Christ's person, but it obviously settled very little.[4] The ensuing centuries saw the Chalcedonian majority within the Byzantine Empire, along with various emperors, struggling to bring monophysites back into communion with the Empire and the Great Church.[5] Out of those struggles came terminological

---

3. Meyendorff, *Christ*, 153, for instance, can recognize the seemingly uncreative, text-book character of *The Orthodox Faith* and yet acknowledge that John Damascene has drawn on the work of his predecessors in such a way that the underlying coherence of their various contributions is revealed. Von Campenhausen, *Fathers*, 175, on the other hand, can speak disparagingly of Byzantine scholasticism and regard John's *Fount of Knowledge* as a "typical combination of cleverness and stupidity."

4. Chesnut, *Christologies*, 3. Her comment here is very much to the point: "It has often been the case that the serious study of Chalcedon has ended with 451, while what came after this is a mere tidying up of loose ends. But the period following the Council cannot be understood in this fashion without giving a truncated and unbalanced picture of Chalcedon itself. No one attempting to make sense of the Arian controversy would stop at 325. In the same way, Chalcedon failed to end the conflict which had its historical beginning with Cyril and Nestorius, and in fact, temporally speaking, *the Council of 451 does not stand at the end of the christological controversies but in the middle.*"

5. Along with Chesnut (see note 4), one can find detailed retellings of this story in

developments that offered solutions to problems left over from earlier councils. John lays these solutions out in clear and comprehensive ways, thereby greatly aiding those who would assess their worth.

John Damascene's achievement deserves continuing study for a second reason. Very little is known of the details of his life, but what can be established reveals a person whose thought developed in the midst of momentous historical circumstances.[6] John was part of a Christian family, the Mansurs, highly placed in the service of the Muslim Caliph of Damascus only a few generations after the death of Muhammed and the relations between Christians and Muslims were not intensely hostile, if not entirely cordial. He seems to have inherited his father's position but, at some point, renounced the world to enter the famous Palestinian monastery of St Sabas (Mar Saba), where Cosmas the Elder, his spiritual father, had preceded him.

There, John poured out a stream of writings, all of which are of continuing interest. Polemics against Islam (and Muhammed in particular), monophysites, and iconoclasts stand next to homilies on the *Theotokos* and liturgical hymns marked by richness and depth. These, along with *The Fount of Knowledge*, reveal a man working in a context of tremendous religious and theological pluralism. They also manifest the ascetical and liturgical mileau of the last decades of John's life. This background of pluralism and prayer needs to inform the approach of those who would interpret the seemingly formal and "scholastic" *Fount*. To read the *Fount* with this context in mind is to allow oneself to be caught up in the urgency and excitement, both historical and personal, of John's time. More importantly, the bewildering complexity of John's historical moment is, in many ways, like our own, so much so that John's life and work can perhaps offer an instructive model for our own groping attempts to find a stable vision in the midst of our pluralistic world.

A third reason for giving close attention to John's achievement is that depth and precision are so often lacking in the way classical doctrinal concepts are appropriated in contemporary theological discussion. All too frequently, traditional words and formulae are invoked in a manner that betrays little understanding of how they actually developed. John's own precision enables us not only to grasp his thought but enter more deeply into his theological tradition as well. As regards *perichoresis*, the careful student

---

Frend, *Rise*; and Florovsky, *Fathers of Sixth to Eighth Century*, esp. 35–190. Still useful is the survey found in Harnack's older but classic *History of Dogma*, 4:226–267.

6. Among the most helpful and accessible sources for the life of John of Damascus are Jugie, "Jean Damascene"; and Kotter's "Johannes von Damaskus," 127–32. A valuable assessment of the various historical claims made on John's behalf can be found in Tsirpanlis's *Anthropology*, 5–20.

can lay claim to a truer and stronger sense of its character in the context of classical doctrine.

The Fount of Knowledge provides the primary locus for the study that follows. In the *Fount*, one finds a whole universe of discourse mapped out and applied. The *Philosophical Chapters* (*Dialectica*), which make up the first of three parts, lay out the categories of being and its various sub-forms in obvious dependence upon Aristotle and his later commentators.[7] Along with precise delineations of words such as substance, accidence, genus, species, we find discussions of such terms as nature, *hypostasis*, and union, which continued into the eighth century and beyond to have christological import both in Chalcedonian and in other churches, whether monophysite or Nestorian. John's explication of these words lays the groundwork for his exposition of *The Orthodox Faith* in the third part of the Fount.

Between the first and last parts of *The Fount of Knowledge* lies a catalogue, *On Heresies* (*Liber de Haersibus*), that, like much of the work as a whole, represents borrowings from earlier sources.[8] What might appear almost as plagiarism to later generations was, for John and his contemporaries, a clear way of standing in continuity with the tradition that had been handed over by faithful teachers from one generation to the next. At least as far back as Cyril of Alexandria, three centuries earlier, pronouncements of recognized guides began to be compiled and used on behalf of controverted viewpoints.[9] John's aim, here as elsewhere, was rarely if ever that of originality.

The list of heresies reveals several interesting things. First, it gives graphic illustration of the pluralism spoken of above. Over a hundred heterodox groups are described, perhaps most of whom still had living embodiment in existing religious communities and were not, therefore, mere repetitions of ancient catalogues.[10] Secondly, it gives clues as to which groups were of most pressing concern to John of Damascus. He provides

---

7. Chase, *Writings*, 7–110. In the notes accompanying his translation of the *Philosophical Chapters*, Chase points out dependence primarily on Aristotle's *Categories*, Ammonius's *In Isagogen* and *In Categorias*, and Porphyry's *Isagoge*.

8. Chase, *Writings*, xxxix, 111–63. He also notes clear dependency on the *Penarion* of Epiphanius. .

9. Von Campenhausen, *Fathers*, 169. He says of Cyril: "He initiated the practice of deciding questions of belief not solely on the basis of the Bible but with the aid of appropriate quotations and collections of quotations from acknowledged authorities and above all the great Athanasius."

10. See Chase, *Writings*, 126; and Kotter, *Schriften*, 4:36. The observation that most of these groups continued to exist in John's day is somewhat conjectural and needs to be substantiated by further investigation. It is based in part on the fact that only one group, the *Angelici*, is said to be extinct. .

only terse description to most of the heresies, but three receive extended comment: the Messalians or Euchites; the monophysites, whom he calls Egyptians and Schematics; and the Muslims, whom he refers to as Saracens and Ishmaelites.[11] These latter groups represent some of the most notable aspects of John's spiritual topography and give the student a glimpse of the character of the eastern Mediterranean world of the eighth century. Thirdly, the list provides an important prelude to John's positive exposition of the faith by pointing out the quagmires and pitfalls he believes lie in wait for those who fail to heed the true tradition.

Having laid out basic definitions and mapped out the territories of wrong opinion, John finally presents his exposition, *The Orthodox Faith*, the longest and historically most important part of *The Fount of Knowledge*. This portion ranges over a whole host of topics, including such things as angels, demons, the heavens, memory, and much more. But most importantly, it has lengthy discussions on the nature of God and the character of the Incarnation. Here, one can find the fruit of centuries of reflection and controversy. Here also, one finds the principal locations for the term, *perichoresis*.

The strategy for the following chapters will be to examine very carefully the whole text of the *Fount*, giving concentrated attention most especially to *The Orthodox Faith*, and trace out the various ways John Damascene allows *perichoresis* to express certain kinds of relationships. The fundamental relationships of the classical doctrine of the Trinity are those of three "persons" (*hypostaseis*) connected to each other in a common "substance" (*ousia*). In the Chalcedonian articulation of the Incarnation, the primary relationship is that of the two "natures" (*physeis*), human and divine, that are united in one "person" (*hypostasis*) in the incarnate Logos. In salvation, understood in an Eastern sense as "deification" (*theosis*), the principal relationship is that of the baptized believer to the sanctified humanity of Christ.

In the case of *theosis*, a new category, participation (identified with various synonyms), will come into play with meanings that overlap, but are by no means identical, with *perichoresis*. But even in connection with the first two doctrines, the Trinity and the Incarnation, none of these relationships are simply interchangeable with the others; each has its own intrinsic character derived from the elements that make up the union.

There is a link, however, that connects the articulation of Trinity and Incarnation. What each of these doctrines shares, for John and the tradition he represents, is the intent to preserve both identity and difference,

---

11. See Chase, *Writings*, 131–37, 138–48, 153–60; and Kotter, *Schriften*, 4:41–48, 49–55, 60–67.

true union and yet intrinsic variety. In each case, the realities making up the relationship are truly "one" reality; at the same time, each element of that one reality retains its own distinctness. So much of ancient doctrinal controversy seems to revolve around ways of expressing the right balance between identity and difference.

That search for the proper balance pushed early theologians in the direction of terminological expansion and refinement because the realities they were attempting to express often seemed to lie beyond the bounds of existing language. The controversy surrounding the Council of Nicea (325 CE) illustrates this. In the theological climate of the time, *ousia* and *hypostasis* were widely regarded as having the same meaning; they were both used to identify the basic "essence" or "substance" underlying any particular existing entity or to refer to "essence" or "substance" in general. Consequently, the use of *homoousios* ("of the same substance") in the creed embraced by the council sounded Sabellian to many and drove them in the direction of one or another form of Arianism. The impasse was not broken until the Cappadocians were able to find a rationale whereby the two terms could be distinguished from each other without the distinguisher falling into either di-theism or tri-theism. The balance between identity and difference was preserved in a way that was convincing to a majority of churches, including those that would later be called Nestorian and monophysite.[12] The christological controversies that followed were not as successful in holding different groups together, but all the antagonists were united in searching for language that would give carefully poised articulation to Christ's incarnate reality.

Perichoresis, as we find it in *The Fount of Knowledge*, is one of the fruits of that search. Like *hypostasis*, it represents a stretching of an existing term to embrace a reality sensed but never adequately articulated. Adequacy is an almost inevitably vague criterion in this context, but a working definition might be that which allows the chief dogmas to be understood even more profoundly in terms of identity and difference. The aim of terminological refinement, for those who would perpetuate an authoritative tradition, is greater clarity, not fundamental doctrinal change.

John Damascene's employment of *perichoresis* as a way of giving greater clarity to the Trinity, the Incarnation, and salvation will be the theme of the next three chapters. The argument of each chapter will attempt to demonstrate that the move toward greater clarity entails a gathering up of

---

12. See Kelly, *Doctrines*, chap. 10, for a concise picture of the achievement of the Cappadocians. Both Nestorians and monophysites accepted the so-called Nicene Creed since each accepted the first and second ecumenical councils.

developing insights that *perichoresis* is able to accomodate. Save in the case of salvation, where the language of participation and communion is more fitting, the notion of mutual indwelling as used by John proves over and over to be elastic enough to embrace that series of moves in post-Chalcedonian debate that strengthened the affirmation of identity and difference in both the Trinity and Christ.

2

Perichoresis and the Trinity

Near the very end of Book One of John Damascene's *Exact Exposition of the Orthodox Faith*, we find this tightly packed statement:

> The abiding and resting of the Persons in one another is not in such a manner that they coalesce or become confused, but, rather, so that they adhere to one another, for they are without interval between them and inseparable and their mutual indwelling [*en allais perichoresin*] is without confusion. For the Son is in the Father and the Spirit, and the Spirit is in the Father and the Son, and Father is in the Son and the Spirit, and there is no merging or blending or confusion. And there is one surge and one movement of the three Persons. It is impossible for this to be found in any created nature.[1]

This chapter will attempt to draw out the character of *perichoresis* in this and other contexts. The goal will be to achieve ever-increasing clarity by viewing the term in its various settings and then reflecting on how it functions in each case. With that end in view, the quotation above serves to provide the basis for some provisional and preliminary analysis.

First of all, note might be made of the fact that *perichoresis* displays its usage in this particular context, not through formal definition but by being placed side by side with qualifying phrases that reveal how the term might be made to work. The "mutual indwelling" of Father, Son, and Spirit is qualified

---

1. Joh.D. *The Orthodox Faith* (hereafter, *OF*) I.14.11–18. I have used Frederic H. Chase Jr.'s translation from *Saint John of Damascus, Writings,* 202. Unless otherwise indicated, I employ Chase's text throughout this and the remaining chapters. At the same time, I have constantly compared it with the Greek text found in the contemporary edition of Kotter, *Schriften,* since Chase had access only to the eighteenth-century edition of Lequien, found in Migne's *Patrologia Graeca,* 94 [hereafter *MPG* 94]. The line reference above (11–18) refer to the Kotter edition.

in two primary ways: the three Persons or (better) *hypostaseis* (*ton trion hypostaseon*—genitive plural) are at the same time "inseparable" (*adiastatoi*) and "without confusion" (*asyngkuton*).[2] Inseparableness is itself qualified by the attribution of "one movement" to the divine triad. *Perichoresis*, at least in this specific instance, seems to entail therefore both the qualities of identity (oneness of place and action) and difference (the continuing separateness of each of the *hypostasteis*.

Another point that the quoted passage makes is that the character of God, with its mutually indwelling *hypostaseis* and singleness of operation, is literally in a class by itself—*sui generis*. The final sentence asserts the impossibility (*adynaton*) of linking the essential features of the divine nature with anything manifested in the created world. What this entails for John's understanding of God will be treated in some depth in a later section dealing with God's relationship to the created world.

Thirdly, I would note that the text under examination gives a glimpse of the growing terminological clarification that was asserted in our first chapter. That assertion will require the whole of this and the following chapter in order to be properly established; but, since it is so central to the entire study, it deserves presentation here in added detail so that it might give focus to the technical discussions that follow.

What I would claim at the outset then is that *perichoresis*, in the above passage, moves Trinitarianism beyond its classic fourth-century formulation to a higher level of conceptual refinement by providing a linguistic vehicle that sums up and becomes the condensed expression of a more sophisticated way of relating identity and difference, a way opened up by the Council of Chalcedon and the debates that followed it in subsequent centuries. Identity and difference as intrinsic to the nature of God had, of course, become a theological commonplace long before the time of John of Damascus. The triumph of Cappadocian Trinitarianism among most groups brought with it the general recognition of fundamental oneness and threeness of God's being.[3] This recognition did not, however, solve all problems. It was still possible, for those who intended to affirm Trinitarian orthodoxy, to fall conceptually into one or another form of modalism, tri-theism, or subordinationism. What was needed was a way to give intelligibility to the

---

2. The last-named term, *asyngkuton*, is drawn from the language of the Chalcedonian Definition. This is crucial for the argument of chapter 2.

3. After the fourth century, the doctrine of the Trinity, as formulated by the Cappadocians and the first two ecumenical councils, became the accepted standard of virtually all the major groups. Later deviations, such as the tritheism of John Philoponus in the sixth century, were rare outside of decidedly sectarian settings. See Prestige, *Patristic Thought*, 282–83; and Meyendorff, *Christ*, 72–73.

relationship of oneness and threeness, identity and difference, so that the mystery could be affirmed without reducing one or the other of the two poles to its opposite.

As our introductory passage from *The Orthodox Faith* makes plain, John Damascene sought for more adequate language in the conceptuality forged in the Chalcedonian and post-Chalcedonian debates. One need only look at the classic formulation of the Fourth Council to see this link. There, there incarnate Son is said to be

> recognized in two natures, without confusion [*asyungkutos*], without change [*atreptos*], without division [*adiairetos*], without separation [*akoristos*]; the distinction of natures being in no way annulled by the union, but rather the characteristics of each nature being preserved and coming together to form one person and subsistence; not as parted or separated into two persons, but one and the same Son and only-begotten God the Word, Lord Jesus Christ . . .[4]

The crucial Chalcedonian adverbs serve to indicate the identity and difference that manifest themselves in the person and nature of Christ. Without collapsing the issues of Trinitarianism into those of Christology, John quite evidently found Chalcedonian language an adequate and useful vehicle for expressing the relation of oneness and threeness in the nature of God. Even though the precise terms are not used in every instance, the vocabulary of separation, merging, blending, confusion and so on throws up the problematics at work in fifth-century christological debate and reveals how new insights generated by one issue can perhaps lead to solutions of problems in other areas.

This preliminary analysis has been directed at a passage I have chosen as a way of introducing the theme of *perichoresis* and the Trinity. But, within John's exposition of the orthodox faith, that passage stands rather as a conclusion, coming as it does at the end of a fourteen-chapter discussion of the nature of God. Those chapters, which came to be known as Book One in the West, present in exacting detail what may or may not be said about God from an early Byzantine perspective. The aim of the remainder of our chapter will be to lay out the scope of Book One and then probe the underlying logic that holds its various parts together. As we probe that logic, our abiding question will be, how does *perichoresis* function here?

John Damascene's masterpiece, *The Orthodox Faith*, was divided by the Latin West into four books of uneven length, broadly in accordance with

---

4. I have used the text found in Bettenson, *Documents*, 73.

the divisions in Peter Lombard's *Sentences*.[5] The present study observes the Western restructuring, including the renumbering of the chapters within each book. This will have the advantage, not only in paralleling the structure of current English translations, but also of bringing out with greater clarity the doctrinal emphases of various parts of *The Orthodox Faith*.

The Scope of Book One

Book One deals exclusively with what can be known and said about God. Chapters 1, 2, and 4 stress the characteristically Greek Christian paradox: God is unknowable and yet can and must be affirmed as Trinity. Chapters 3, 5, 6, and 7 offer rational considerations for those unable to accept the Christian God on the basis of faith. Chapter 8, the centerpiece of Book One, is a relatively lengthy disquisition on the character of the Holy Trinity. The remaining chapters, 9 through 14, extend the discussion of the relationship of the divine attributes to God's unknowability. All in all, Book One comprises a fairly comprehensive doctrinal exposition of God's nature, although little is done to show the connections between the individual *hypostaseis* and the work of salvation. Despite certain omissions, one could merely summarize these chapters in order and present a reasonably clear picture of a major portion of John Damascene's thought.

The following study aims at more than simple exposition. The goal of this and the following chapters, as stated in the introduction, is the double one of gaining greater clarity about John's employment of the term *perichoresis* and grasping with greater depth his manner of presenting God, Christ, and salvation. The quest for clarity cannot be fully understood apart from the presentations of doctrine that form the contexts in which *perichoresis* is found; the doctrinal expositions (we will contend) lack something in focus and coherence apart from an understanding of *perichoresis*. The task then of this chapter and what follows is to push beneath the surface structure and uncover networks of interconnected ideas that provide the vital context of *perichoresis* and are in turn held together by it.

The Inner Logic of John Damascene's Trinitarian Theology

Intrinsic to any theological use of the term *perichoresis*, regardless of the context, is some sort of relationship. The very words used in the search to

---

5. Chase, *Writings*, xxxii.

find English equivalents (e.g., mutual indwelling, interpenetration, coinherence, and so on) imply a connection between at least two terms. Whether we are dealing with two natures or three *hypostaseis*, *perichoresis* is one of the available words that can be used to identify the particular relationship involved.

Throughout this section, relationship, both in the sense of *perichoresis* and in a much wider sense, will be used to organize our analysis. What follows can be grouped broadly under two categories: God's relationship to the created world; and God's internal relationships. An understanding of the former category throws the latter into sharper relief.

God's Relationship to the Created World

The passage from *The Orthodox Faith* that was chosen to open this chapter underscores the cleavage that John Damascene claims exists between God's nature and that of created beings. The "mutual indwelling" (*perichoresin*) that characterizes the members of the Holy Trinity surpasses what is possible (*adynaton*) for human beings and all other creatures.[6] More than that, as other passages will attest, it is fundamentally unthinkable.[7]

If such is indeed the case, however, we might well ask how *perichoresis* in relation to the Trinity can be known or spoken of in any degree whatsoever. At this point, analogy can be invoked. Theology has traditionally worked with some notion of analogy, but analogy necessarily assumes a real, though perhaps intuited, connection between the realities compared. Lacking that connection, analogical language would collapse into meaningless syllables. That something more that empty nonsense may underlie John's thought here will now be discussed in relation to two staples of early Byzantine theology: revelation and *apophasis*.

Theology within the Limits of Revelation

The opening chapter of Book One of *The Orthodox Faith* is crucial to all that follows. At first glance, it might appear to be a *pro forma* nod in the direction of Holy Scripture and authoritative teachers before getting on with the business at hand. Sacred tradition, specifically in its canonical form as Scripture, is acknowledged as foundational to what follows.[8] A closer scrutiny reveals,

---

6. Joh.D. *OF* I.14.13,18 (trans. Chase, 202).

7. This point is made with great emphasis in the first chapter of Book One of *OF*; see also the assertions found in I.4 (trans. Chase, 170–72).

8. I use sacred tradition here, and throughout the text, primarily in an Eastern

however, that John's introductory statement is not merely conventional and perfunctory. On the basis of Scripture, knowledge of God as Trinity is itself declared to have a Trinitarian origin. That is, each of the *hypostaseis* of the Trinity plays an indispensable role in revealing one or both of the other two. Furthermore, apart their revelations of each other, no knowledge of God is claimed to be available beyond that of God's bare existence. Two scriptural quotations, plus a paraphrase of a third, frame John's assertions. In their full form, these are:

> No one has ever seen God; the only Son, who is in the bosom of the Father, he has made him known. John 1:18

> All things have been delivered to me by my Father; and no one knows the Son except the Father, and no one knows the Father except the Son and anyone to whom the Son chooses to reveal him. Matthew 11:27

> For what person knows a man's thoughts except the spirit of that man which is in him? So also, no one comprehends the thoughts of God except the Spirit of God. I Corinthians 2:11[9]

John introduces these texts to establish that God is "ineffable, inexpressible" (*arraton*) and "beyond comprension" (*akatalapton*). Although there was a "natural" knowledge given to the first humans, that knowledge ("after the first and blessed nature"—*Meta de tan protan kai markarian physin*) has been lost and not even the angels (*cheroubim, seraphim*) possess it.[10] What that original knowledge actually entailed is not spelled out, but the whole drift of John's thought suggests that what the first humans knew (before sin) still did not penetrate the depths of incomprehensibility.

John immediately qualifies God's incomprehensible character in two ways already indicated above. As regards the first way, he can say:

> Nevertheless, God has not gone so far as to leave us in complete ignorance, for through nature the knowledge of the existence of God has been revealed by Him to all . . . The very creation with

---

Christian sense as referring broadly to Scripture and its authoritative interpretation by accredited Fathers and councils; see Lossky, "Tradition and Traditions," in *Image*, 141–68; and Prestige, "Tradition: or, The Scriptural Basis of Theology: A Prologue," in *Fathers*, 1–22.

9. Joh.D. *OF* I.1.1–10 (trans. Chase, 165).

10. Joh.D. *OF* I.1.2, 10–13 (trans. Chase, 165).

> its ordering and harmony proclaims the majesty of the divine nature.[11]

The background here is obviously provided by a key passage like Romans 1:19–20, along with the tradition of Logos theology, and John's assertions are as terse and undeveloped as Paul's. They do claim emphatically though that there is a natural (*physikos*) knowledge of God's existence (*tou einai Theon*) and that that knowledge entails a revelation of God's majesty (*megaleion*).

As the next three chapters of Book One make manifestly clear, however, knowledge of God's existence and majesty does not constitute knowledge of God's inner being.[12] That remains fundamentally unknowable, although the second qualification, now to be mentioned, provides something of a limiting framework for what at first might seem to be an illimitable notion.

What gives limited comprehensibility to the incomprehensibe, for John Damascene, is the revelation that each of the *hypostaseis* of the Trinity discloses about the inner character of the Godhead. The three scriptural passages quoted above indicate the basis of such a claim. Each *hypostasis* is able to reveal because each speaks, as it were, from the inside. And what each reveals, according to the passages cited, is one or more of the other *hypostaseis*, though not necessarily the one making the revelation. The structure of the revelatory movement might be as follows:

> The Son alone has seen the Father.
> The Father alone has known the Son
> The Son alone can reveal the Father.
> The Father alone can (presumably) reveal the Son.
> The Spirit of God knows God's thoughts.
> The Spirit: God :: the human spirit : the human person

At this point, the relationship of the Spirit's knowledge to what the other *hypostaseis* "alone" know is not developed. Later, especially in chapter 8 of Book One, John affirms the the common "operation" of all three *hypostaseis* in a way that gives added intelligibility to the above progression. Here, that progression functions as part of the assertion that there is no "natural" knowledge of God apart from that of God's existence and majesty. No suggestion is made, at least in chapter 1 of Book One, that the Son, as the Logos informing the created order, somehow provides access to the true and full nature of the Godhead through "natural" reason. Instead, John presents us with a seemingly unbridgeable chasm between God and creation that has nevertheless been spanned, in a partial yet sufficient way, from the side of

---

11. Joh.D. *OF* I.1.14–17 (trans. Chase, 165–66).
12. Joh.D. *OF* I.4.1–2, 22–25 (trans. Chase, 170–71)

God. That limited but real knowledge of God, a knowledge that goes beyond God's existence and majesty, comes to us from two sources:

> Indeed, He has given us knowledge of Himself in accordance with our capacity, at first [*proteron*] through the Law and the Prophets [*dia nomou de kai prophaton*] and then afterwards [*epeita*] through his only begotten Son, our Lord and God and Savior, Jesus Christ [*tou monogenous autou huiou, kyriou de kai theou kai soteros hamon, Iasou Christou*].[13]

Here John draws a line. Beyond the two stages of God's self-revelation, he does not look for a third stage, at least in this life, that might cast what has been given us in a wholly new light. The sacred tradition, that which has been handed over (*paradedomena*), marks out the limits beyond which one neither can nor should attempt to go:

> Accordingly, we accept all those things that have been handed down by the Law and the Prophets and the Apostles and the Evangelists, and we know and revere them, and over and above these things we seek nothing else.[14]

To work within the confines of sacred scripture is a methodological principle that John sees as required by the nature of the God revealed therein. Apart from that self-revelation, even the little that has been manifested in the canon ("in accordance with our capacity") would remain beyond reach.

The underlying thrust of chapter 1 of Book One can now be summarized as follows. According to John Damascene, God's nature is fundamentally unknowable. The created order confirms God's basic existence, but beyond that such knowledge as humans may receive is found in the canonical scriptures (as interpreted by authoritative teachers), preeminently in their witness to the Son. Through the manifestation of the Son and his revelation of the Father and bestowal of the Spirit, all that can be known is given to us. God remains beyond our reach but must be grasped in a Trinitarian way. Father, Son, and Spirit provide the necessary entry point into a reality that must remain permanently incomprehensible.

Apophasis and the Limits of Creation

The next three chapters of Book One explore the character of God's unknowability. The tradition of "negative theology" (*apophasis*) that Byzantine theology inherited most notably from Gregory of Nyssa and Pseudo-Dionysius

13. Joh.D. *OF* I.1.17–19 (trans. Chase, 166)
14. Joh.D. *OF* I.1.19–22 (trans. Chase, 166).

occupied John's thought as well.[15] That tradition tended to place the ultimate character of God's being beyond the reach of human speech. God's inner nature is in such stark contrast to God's creation that one can only use the elements of created existence in a contrastive way: they assist in showing us what God is not. As to what God is, positively, even what can be affirmed in dogma merely takes us to the threshold of ultimate mystery.

At first glance, the apophatic tradition might seem to stand in opposition to two other traditions. For one, it might seem in conflict with the scriptural tradition itself, with its assertions and narrative indications about God's reality. How John, along with most other authoritative interpreters of classic Eastern Christian thought, would respond to such a charge will be clarified by the discussion of begetting and creating later in this same sub-section.

Secondly, the apophatic stance might also seem to be in conflict with the broad philosophical tradition of the ancient world or at least that part of it that viewed the cosmos as ultimately accessible to the (purified) human mind.[16] The prevailing assumption of most schools that the world (*kosmos*) was self-contained and self-explanatory clashed in the strongest possible way with the Christian (and Jewish) understanding of creation, an understanding whose revolutionary impact has been thoroughly explored by Georges Florovsky and others.[17] John Damascene works out the theological implications of such a belief, not only in the chapters mentioned above but throughout Book One. His most important discussion comes in the crucial chapter 8.

Chapter 8 of Book One of *The Orthodox Faith* is the section devoted expressly to the three *hypostaseis* of the Holy Trinity and will therefore be

---

15. Useful analyses of Gregory and Dionysius in relation to *apophasis* can be found in Louth, *Origins*, 80–97, 159–78; see also the discussion of Evagrius (100–113), whose influence on mainstream Byzantine religious thought was made possible by his work being attributed to others. Lossky also provides probing studies of apophatic theology, especially as it relates to Dionysius, in "Apophasis and Trinitarian Theology," *Image*, 13–29; and *Mystical Theology*, 23–43.

16. I am obviously excluding the various skeptical traditions that existed side by side with the optimism of most of the various heirs of Plato and Aristotle; see Armstrong, *Ancient Philosophy*, 138–140. For a clear understanding of the thought world of the prevailing schools of philosophy in the ancient world, see (along with Armstrong) Allen, *Understanding*, Introduction and chaps. 1–5.

17. Florovsky's essay "St. Athanasius' Concept of Creation" has been reprinted in his *Aspects*, 39–62. Two other studies, remarkable for their clarity, are Allen's "Introduction: the Foundation of Christian Theology: The World Was Created," in *Understanding*, 1–14; and Armstrong's opening chapter ("God, and the World; Creation") in Armstrong and Markus, *Christian Faith*, 1–7.

central to the analysis of God's internal relationships that form the second half of our own chapter. The present discussion will anticipate some of that analysis by way of explicating the teaching on creation. The two discussions, are of necessity intertwined because John's view of creation arises in the context of his setting forth the relationship of the Father and the Son.

For John Damascene, as for the orthodox tradition generally since Athanasius, Father and Son are related to each other as begetter and begotten.[18] He explains begetting by contrasting it to creating and making:

> On the one hand, begetting [*gennasis*] is a bringing forth of the essence [*ousias*] of the one begetting [*gennotos*] a child [*gennomenon*] similar [*homoion*] to the being of the parent. On the other hand, creation [*ktisis*] or making [*poiasis*] is of something external [*exothen*] to the one creating, something created and made completely unlike [*anomoian pantelos*].[19]

The contrast set forth here is stark and could be construed as a concise commentary on those phrases of the Niceno-Constantinopolitan Creed that read: "... begotten, not made, being of one substance of the Father, through whom all things were made."[20]

At this point in our study, John's distinction between creating and begetting serves to underscore the gap already noted between God and the world. From the perspective of Nicene theology, the gap exists because creation comes forth, not out of God's own substance but is made out of nothing and is therefore out of that which is not God. A pervasive philosophical principle of the ancient world was that "like knows like."[21] That principle underlay the confidence of many of the schools that human minds could penetrate the *nous* or *logos* lying behind the phenomenal world because the two, human reason and ultimate reality, were believed to be fundamentally united. No such confidence exists in John; creatures, even creatures created in God's image, do not have an immediacy or fullness of access to the deepest levels of reality because the difference between creation and begottenness is qualitative. John's use of Paul's words in I Corinthians 2:11 should

---

18. All of whom draw, no doubt, ultimately on the Fourth Gospel, where *monogenas* is a key term.

19. Joh.D. *OF* I.8.58-62; my translation (cf. trans. Chase, 178-79).

20. Such is the current ecumenical translation found, among other places, in the 1979 (American) *Book of Common Prayer*.

21. Again, Allen, *Understanding*, is instructive here. The reader is urged to examine this notion in the wider context of ancient philosophy generally, where numerous theories of knowledge presuppose a real measure of identity between knower and known.

be recalled: "No one comprehends the thoughts of God except the Spirit of God."

As Georges Florovsky has brilliantly demonstrated, the distinction between creating and begetting that John inherited as part of his tradition goes back to Athanasius and the early battle with Arianism.[22] According to Florovsky, Athanasius faced in Arius a kind of reversed Origenism. Origen wrestled with the problem that a creation in time would pose for God's immutability. Like virtually all early Christian thinkers, he accepted immutability as an unquestioned given.[23] For God to be mutable would mean that the highest reality was open to forces of change that might significantly alter the character of that reality.

Where Origen ran into difficulty, from the standpoint of a later orthodoxy, is that he confused ontological and cosmological questions.[24] He was convinced that the Son was eternally begotten of the Father because God must always be Father or else be mutable. By the same reasoning, Origen assumed that God must always be Creator and the world must likewise be eternal.[25] Arius reversed this move. Standing Origenism on its head, he rejected the eternity of both the world and the Logos. What both teachers shared in common was the attempt to place the problem of God in a cosmological framework.[26]

According to Florovsky, Athanasius likewise wrestled with the problem of creation but was able to move beyond the impasse posed by Origen. He did so by restructuring the argument in such a way that he could envision for the Logos a role independent of creation. For Arius, the Logos as the agent of creation first had to be created itself. Even as the "first-born," it remained on the side of the created world in the permanent cleavage that existed between Creator and created. Athanasius drew the line differently. For him, the Logos was on the side of God in the division separating that which is eternal and unchanging from that which is temporal. As such, the Logos would have had that character, regardless of whether the world had ever been created or should cease to exist.[27] The affirmation Athanasius makes is clear: "Even supposing that the Father had never been disposed

---

22. Florovsky, "Athanasius," in *Creation*, 39–62.

23. A helpful orientation to immutability can be found in Bondi's "Immutability," in *The Westminster Dictionary of Christian Theology*, eds. Richardson and Bowden, 288.

24. Florovsky, "Athanasius," 42–44.

25. Ibid., 42–44.

26. Ibid., 46–48.

27. Ibid., 51.

to create the world, or a part of it, nevertheless the Logos would have with God and the Father with him. . . ."[28] By reframing the basic relationships of God, the Logos, and creation, Athanasius was able to affirm the eternity of the Word and the temporality of the world in such a way that the eternal character of God could accommodate them both. Neither Word nor world brings about an alternation of God's basic nature. The Logos is intrinsic to the divine nature and is therefore in a real sense necessary; the creation exists by virtue of the divine will and is, therefore, contingent and, strictly speaking, unnecessary.[29]

With Origen then, Athanasius could affirm the eternity of the Word but broke with him over the eternity of creation and the ontologically subordinate character of the Word (and Spirit). With Arius, Athanasius could affirm the time-bound nature of the world but could not accept the creatureliness of the Logos. His position, as presented by Florovsky, might be set forth as follows:

| Logos | eternal | begotten of God's own being |
| World | temporal | created of God's own will |

It should be pointed out that Athanasius provides an illustration here of the process of terminological clarification we have spoken of before. The ground he gained, the distinctions he laid down in the struggle with Arianism, became part of the permanent legacy of the Byzantine (and Latin) Church. What appears to have made Athanasius's achievement possible was an underlying rationale whereby God could both create and beget without God's immutable nature being altered.

It is entirely within the boundaries of this rationale that John Damascene lays out his own exposition. Speaking out of the Athanasian/Cappadocian tradition, he can affirm that "neither begetting nor creating alters the one, untouched, unwavering, invariable and always constant God."[30] Since God's being is outside time (*akronos*) and has no beginning (*anarchos*), it does not bring about some temporal alteration in that being. God's being is always begetting and is therefore, in this respect, changeless.[31] And since creation is the work of God's will (*thelaseos ergon*), it is not co-internal (*ou synaidos*) with God and therefore not out of God's true nature.[32]

---

28. Athanasius, *Contra Arianos* II.31; quoted in Florovsky, "Athanasius," 51–52.
29. Florovsky, "Athanasius," 51–53.
30. Joh.D. *OF* I.8.63–64; my translation. Cf. Chase, *Writings*, 179.
31. Joh.D. *OF* I.8.70 (trans. Chase, 179).
32. Joh.D. *OF* I.8.70 (trans. Chase, 179).

Earlier, the sharp contrast between God's being and the created world was noted. Since creating and begetting are also human activities, we should examine the analogical link that appears to tie God and humanity together at certain points. *Apophasis* might suggest that analogy is a closed door here, but John can affirm both ultimate mystery and analogical overlap. As regards creating, he has this to say:

> Indeed, God and man do not make in the same way. Thus man does not bring anything from non-being into being. What man makes, he makes from already existing material, not just by willing but by thinking it out beforehand and getting an idea of what he is to make and then working with his hands, toiling and troubling and oftentimes failing because the object of his endeavor does not turn out as he wished. God, on the other hand, has brought all things from nothing into being by the mere act of his will.[33]

Likewise, human and divine begetting have important (and expressable) differences:

> Hence, God and man do not beget in the same way. For, since God is without time and without beginning, unaffected, unchanging, incorporeal, unique, and without end, He begets without time and without beginning, unaffectedly, unchangingly, and without copulation.[34]

Humanity, by contrast, works within a whole set of limitations from which God is free:

> Now it is obvious that [the human person] begets in quite a different manner, since he is subject to birth and death and flux and increase, and since he is clothed with a body and has male and female in his nature—for the male has need of the female's help.[35]

The apophatic character of what John asserts is not dissolved by analogy because God's uniqueness and ultimate mystery are highlighted, by way of contrast, with what can be said positively of God's being and activity.

What enabled John Damascene and his predecessors in the apophatic tradition to use any analogy at all was the language of Scripture. Scripture authorized John to conclude, on the basis of revelation, a whole host of

---

33. Joh.D. *OF* I.8.72–78 (trans. Chase, 179).
34. Joh.D. *OF* I.8.79–82 (trans. Chase, 179).
35. Joh.D. *OF* I.8.89–94 (trans. Chase, 179).

things about God, including God's unbeginningness (*anarchos*), uncreatedness (*aktistos*), and bodilessness (*asomatos*).³⁶ He can further assert that God is of one substance (*mia ousia*) and in three "persons" (*en trisin hypostasesi*). He can go on to claim knowledge of the incarnate Word, his miraculous birth, and his perfect divinity (*theos teleios*) and perfect humanity (*anthropos teleios*).³⁷ He can say much else besides. But when John returns to the question of God's basic essence (*ousia*) or how the Son emptied (*kenosas*) himself in the economy of the incarnation, unknowability once again thrusts itself into the picture. Faced with God's ultimate nature, we can neither know nor say (*agnooumen kai legein oute dynametha*).³⁸

Scripture, then, both reveals and conceals. Either in its own language or in the language derived from it, it falls short of reaching full expression of who or what God ultimately is. Unknowability, therefore, extends right into the heart of revelation itself.

Since the qualitative chasm between God and the world is only partially bridged by what has been revealed, what status then do biblical terms or theological terms derived from the Bible have? Scripture is full of characterizations of divine being. God is said to be living, powerful, holy, just, righteous, merciful, jealous, wrathful, and so on. John Damascene accepts these, of course, but resists any interpretation of them that would regard God as fundamentally and essentially composed of different things and, therefore, compounded (*diaphoron syngkeimenon syntheton estin*).³⁹ John's positive response is as follows:

> The Divine is simple and uncompounded. But, that which is composed of several different things is compounded. Consequently, should we say that the increate, unoriginate, incorporeal, immortal, eternal, good, creative, and the like are essential differences in God, then, since He is composed of so many things, He will not be simple but compounded which is impious to the last degree. Therefore, one should not suppose that any one of these things which are affirmed of God are indicative of what He is in essence. Rather, they show either what he is not, or some relation to some one of those things which are consequential to His nature or operation.⁴⁰

---

36. Joh.D. *OF* I.2.10–15 (trans. Chase, 167). See also OF I.8.1–23 (trans. Chase, 176–77).

37. Joh.D. *OF* I.2.16–31 (trans. Chase, 167–68).

38. Joh.D. *OF* I.2.31–38 (trans. Chase, 168).

39. Joh.D. *OF* I.9.1–2 (trans. Chase, 189).

40. Joh.D. *OF* I.9.1–13 (trans. Chase, 189).

John's answer is basically two-fold. Such terms either indicate what God is not, or they point to relationships created by what God is or what God has done. The former are represented by various negative designations whereby God is claimed to be not finite, not created, not temporal, without a body, and so on. Each of these offers a contrast to what is familiar to us in the created world; none has a positive content that can be imagined within the terms of created existence. All transcend the limits that many of the philosophical schools of the ancient world regarded as essential to even partial knowledge.[41]

The second part of John's response points to those relationships that follow (*parepomenon*) from God's nature (*physei*) or activity (*energeian*). This element in John's thought hints at, leaving undeveloped, a distinction that goes back to Gregory of Nyssa but had to wait until the fourteenth century for its fullest development.[42] That distinction, which has since come to be associated with the name of Gregory Palamas and the Hesychast controversy from which he emerged as the hero of late Byzantine theology and spirituality, drew a line between God's essence and God's energies (or operations), whereby things could be attributed to the energies that could not, strictly speaking, be said of the essence, even though God's operations truly reflected and embodied who God is.[43] The distinction provided a rationale wherein God could be seen to interact with the world in such a way that the divine essence remains undisturbed. Even though John does not give extended treatment to this line of thinking, it surely finds implicit expression in John's treatment of creating and begetting, neither of which alters God's nature, because the former is a manifestation of God's will external to God and the latter is an eternal aspect of God's internal being and likewise bespeaks of no structural alteration of that being.[44]

We might pause at this point to ask if John's thought does not represent a sort of anticipation of deism or, perhaps, nominalism. The gap between God and the world is so wide that connection between the two, apart from the initial act of creation and the Incarnation might seem almost non-existent. Furthermore, the world, created as it is out of God's uncoerced freedom, bespeaks of a creator but does not provide a mirror reflecting God's

---

41. The reader is again referred to the volumes of Armstrong and Allen mentioned above (in notes 16 and 17). For more detailed treatment, *Cambridge History of Late Greek and Early Medieval Philosophy*, ed. Armstrong, should be consulted.

42. Joh.D. *OF* I.9.7–9 (trans. Chase, 189). For an incisive treatment of the later controversies with frequent allusions to earlier figures, see Meyendorff, *Palamas*.

43. There is a growing body of literature to clarify the complexities of this issue. In addition to Meyendorff, a helpful survey article is Every's "Hesychasm," 73–91.

44. Joh.D. *OF* I.8.79–82 (trans. Chase, 179).

inner being. In either case, there is no way of reasoning backwards from creation to the character of God's *ousia*.

To tie John, even tenuously, to either of these later movements is to miss an important dimension in his own thought. God, even apart from redemptive intervention represented preeminently by the Incarnation, continues to be pervasively present in the created order, sustaining and perfecting it. God is said to be not only

> maker of all things both visible and invisible, [but also] holding together all things and conserving them, provider for all, governing and dominating and ruling over all in unending and immortal reign; without contradiction, filling all things [*panta plarousan*], contained by nothing, but Himself containing all things . . . ; pervading all substances without being defiled . . .[45]

This statement, in chapter 8 of Book One of *The Orthodox Faith*, has its parallel in the earlier claims of chapter 4 of the same book, where John maintains that God "permeates" (*hakein*) and "fills" (*plaroun*) all things.[46]

As their larger contexts make plain, these statements serve both to link God and the world and, at the same time, to illustrate their qualitative difference. The passage from chapter 4 of Book One underscores the point. After claiming that God permeates and fills all on the basis of a passage from Jeremiah, John proceeds to ask how that is possible given the impossibility (*adynaton*) of one body permeating another body (*soma dia somaton diakein*) without having its own integrity violated.[47] His reasoning here is essentially Aristotelian, as the remainder of John's paragraph makes plain:

> But, since everything that is moved is moved by another, then who is it that moves this? And who is it that moves that? And so we go on endlessly in this way until such time as we arrive at something that is immovable. For the first mover is unmoved, and it is just this that is the Divinity. Furthermore, how can that which is not locally contained be moved? Therefore, only the Divinity is unmoved, and by His immovability He moves all things [*di' akinasias ta panta kinoun*].[48]

The notion of a prime cause, an unmoved mover, that is bodiless and can affect without being affected in return, uses both the language and conceptuality of Aristotle. That conceptuality is elsewhere qualified in highly

---

45. Joh.D. *OF* I.8–15 (trans. Chase, 176–77).
46. Joh.D. *OF* I.4.9 (trans. Chase, 171).
47. Joh.D. *OF* I.4.10–13 (trans. Chase, 171).
48. Joh.D. *OF* I.4.17–21 (trans. Chase, 171).

significant ways, most especially by affirmations of God's purposeful involvement with creation. What deserves to be stressed here, however, is that God's very engagement with the world is of such a nature as to reveal the wide chasm separating the two. The reason that God's reality can embrace everything else without being affected is that the two exist on entirely different planes. The created order exists at the behest of God's will and is therefore contingent on the realm that transcends it, but the relationship is not reciprocal: the world cannot exert a corresponding influence on God.[49] Our next chapter, on the Incarnation, will qualify this statement in interesting ways, but for now it must stand as it is.

Vladimir Lossky has reminded us that theology, as understood by most ancient Christian thinkers, focused on the eternal and transcendent nature of God and not on God's activity either in creation or redemption.[50] Since *perichoresis* is language that purports to indicate something meaningful about God's essential character, one might well ask why so much space has been devoted to discussing God's relationship to creation. Two points can be made in response.

First, since anything said about the God of the Bible necessarily entails analogical speech, it has been important to show from the perspective of John Damascene from whence that language may or may not be derived. For John, the various metaphors and abstractions, positive and negative, that cumulatively reveal who God is, both internally and in relation to us, may be of common coin in most instances but receive their theological value by being funded with meaning derived from divine revelation as interpreted by tradition. John looks to prophets, apostles, and evangelists, each of whom bore witness to the supreme revelation, the incarnate Son, for whatever can be said about God.

By contrast, the creation, apart from the focus that revelation gives it, is a barren source, at least since the Fall.[51] True, some arguments for the Trinity derived from reason are given, especially in chapters 6 and 7 of Book One; but these have merely a kind of retrospective weight for those who already share certain Christian presuppositions and are half-inclined to embrace a full-blown Christian understanding of God.[52]

---

49. The implication here is that the spiritual can affect the physical but not the other way around—unless, however, the spiritual and the physical are combined in one being, with different results, we might assume, for ordinary human beings and the incarnate Son.

50. Lossky, *Image*, 15. He distinguishes between *theologia* and *oikonomia*, the latter referring to the Incarnation in contrast to God's eternal being.

51. See Joh.D. *OF* I.1 (trans. Chase, 165–66); and I.8.165–71 (trans. Chase, 183).

52. See Joh.D. *OF* I.6–7 (trans. Chase, 174–76) where reflection on what is implied

Perichoresis *and the Trinity*   25

Perichoresis, then, along with other technical terms used to give expression to the mystery of the Trinity, finds its ultimate source in revelation, though it has other, non-theological uses.[53] The whole history of that tradition of which John Damascene is a part, that group of thinkers stretching from Athanasius and the Cappadocians through the various defenders of Chalcedon, including Maximus the Confessor, struggled against the unwanted implications of certain terms, not necessarily by abandoning the terms themselves but by investing them with revised meanings controlled by what had been received as the truth of revelation.[54] The separation of *ousia* and *hypostasis*, mentioned in our introductory chapter, illustrates this tendency well.[55] The value, then, of the discussion of the last several pages is, one would hope, that it has clarified the basis on which John's theological assertions are made. For John, revelation employs the language of creation (what other language is there?) but uses it both to express truths that the mind unaided would never discover and to point to realities that lie beyond the power of any language to express. As the opening section of the *Fount of Knowledge* amply shows, John has no hesitancy in "plundering the wealth of Egypt" in his borrowing of philosophical terms and concepts. Indeed, he cites the Scripture that says, "Every good and perfect gift is from above," as justification.[56] But he constantly stretches language to the limits of its conventional usages and strains after that which he believes lies beyond all language.

Before making our second point, we should note that the apophatic character of John's thought has a somewhat different quality from that of some of his illustrious predecessors. One finds in Gregory of Nyssa and, especially, Pseudo-Dionysius a tendency to move ever more deeply into the realm of unknowability, whether that be seen as ever-brighter light or ever-increasing darkness.[57] The mystical, trans-verbal strain is not nearly so

---

by the language of word, spirit, breath, and so on in human experience is applied to the same language as descriptive of God.

53. For various non-theological uses, see the classic studies of Prestige, *Patristic Thought*, 282–301; "Perichorero and Perichoresis, " 242–52. For additional data on how *perichoresis* has functioned in various contexts, see Deneffe, "*Perichoresis*," 497–532.

54. See the analysis of Florovsky, "Revelation, Philosophy, and Theology," in *Creation*, 21–40.

55. Fourth-century developments found it expedient to separate these virtually synonymous terms, allowing *hypostasis* to take on the meaning of personal or individual and leaving *ousia* to designate a common nature.

56. Jas 1:17

57. The reader is referred to the works of Louth and Lossky cited in note 15 above.

pronounced in John. He acknowledges God's unknowability but counsels contentment with what has been revealed in the Old and New Testaments:

> Since therefore He [God] knows all things and provides for each in accordance with his needs, He has revealed to us what it is expedient for us to know, whereas that which we were unable to bear He has withheld. With these things let us not step over the ancient bounds or pass beyond the divine tradition.[58]

Pseudo-Dionysius, on the other hand, often appears to want to leave behind even Trinitarian language, with all its mystery-laden meaning, as if it too were a transitory and finally inadequate representation of God's being. Rowan Williams cites certain passages in *The Divine Names* (*De Divinis Nominibus*) that suggest that the "persons" of the Trinity are in fact emanations of the primal unity and that God is neither "three" nor "one" but is beyond all such characterizations. In II.4, we find:

> For . . . the Initiates of our Divine Tradition designate the Undifferenced Attributes of the Transcendently Ineffable and Unknowable Permanence as hidden, incommunicable Ultimates, but the beneficent Differentiations of the Supreme Godhead, they call emanations [*proodus te kai ekphanseis*] and Manifestations. . . .[59]

In XIII.3, we read:

> And hence, when we speak of the All-Transcendent Godhead as an Unity and a Trinity, It is not an Unity or a Trinity such as can be known by us or any creature, though to express the truth of Its utter Self-Union and Its Divine Fecundity we apply the titles "Trinity" and "Unity" to That which is beyond Being. But no Unity or Trinity or Number of Oneness or Fecundity or any other other thing that either is a creature or can be known to any creature, is able to utter the mystery, beyond all mind and reason, of that Transcendent Godhead which super-essentially surpasses all things.[60]

On the basis of passages such as these, Rowan Williams makes this assessment: "It is hard to avoid the conclusion that Dionysius does indeed consider the Trinity to be part of the divine dispensation rather than the

---

58. Joh.D. *OF* I.1.24–28 (trans. Chase, 166).
59. Dion, Ar., *D.n.* II.4 (trans. Rolt, 69).
60. Dion.Ar., *D.n.* XIII.3 (trans. Rolt, 188).

intrinsic divine reality."[61] Andrew Louth would qualify this reading somewhat but notes the same tendency.[62] Vladimir Lossky, on the other hand, can take the text noted above that denies both oneness and threeness to God as final testimony to the incomprehensible character of the Triune God.[63] In either case, the cautious restraint of John Damascene, the willingness to keep within the boundaries laid out in the established reading of Scripture, finds few parallels in the efforts of Dionysius to push beyond the limits of language on the basis of *apophasis*.

A second reason for dwelling at length on God's relationship to the world is that, while *perichoresis* in a Trinitarian context refers to what is beyond creation, the same term is used by John to express other relationships as well, most especially that of Christ's two natures. It can also bear a related, though ultimately contrasting, meaning to words expressing the relation of humans to God in salvation as well as words cited above indicating God's providential presence in the governance of the world. Our discussion of creation, therefore, can be used both to sharpen the contrast between what can be said on the basis of revelation about God's inner nature and what can be known and said apart from that revelation and to provide the setting for God's revelation of divine being in the Incarnation and salvation. In the latter case, it should be pointed out that creation, like Scripture itself, both conceals and makes manifest certain realities, a point that will gain added meaning in chapter 3. Now, we need to explicate *perichoresis* in the context of the ontological Trinity.

God's Inner Relations

As was noted earlier, the crucial locus of John Damascene's understanding of the Holy Trinity is chapter 8 of Book One of *The Orthodox Faith*. There, in the midst of a lengthy disavowal that God is either three gods or one person, John asserts that the *hypostaseis* of the Trinity

> . . . are united [*henountai*] . . . so as not to be confused [*syncheisthai*], but to hold fast [*echesthai*] to one another, and they have their mutual indwelling [*perichoresin*] in one another without blending [*synaloiphas*] or being kneaded together [*symphyrseos*] [and] without change [*oude existamenon*] or cutting

---

61. Williams, *Christian Spirituality*, 120.
62. Louth, *Origin*, 159–78.
63. Lossky, *Mystical Theology*, 43.

apart [*temnomenon*] of the essence in the manner of Arius's division [*diairesin*].[64]

As with the passage used to introduce our present chapter, these words entail the use of the term *perichoresis* (*perichoresin*) and establish a clear context for determining how the word can be made to function in relation to the Trinity. Once again, the conceptuality and some of the actual language of Chalcedon are employed to lay out the character of both identity and distinction in the divine nature.

Lest John be thought guilty of some kind of category mistake here, of using distinctions appropriate for one issue to explicate a different issue, we can remind ourselves that both Trinity and Incarnation involve the notion of relationship, even though the entities being related are distinct. In this connection, an earlier point bears repeating: each doctrine has a stake in preserving both identity and difference. This is not to suggest that to define the nature of *perichoresis* in connection with either one of these doctrines is automatically to define it for the other one as well, because each has features uniquely its own. But Chalcedon provided language for expressing how things brought together in union could nevertheless remain distinct. It was natural then that terms used to clarify the character of identity and difference in Christology should be used to address the same problem in theology.

In chapter 3 below, which focuses on the issue of Christ's person, we will note a reciprocal move in which Trinitarian distinctions come into play to shed light on the problem of two wills and two energies or operations in the incarnate Word. In the present chapter, we will explore divine personhood in terms of identity and difference, comparing and contrasting it with examples from created existence, and then place *perichoresis* in the context of the whole chapter in order to assess what light it sheds and what light is shed upon it.

Identity and Difference in the Trinity

In its simplest terms, John Damascene's affirmation of the identity and difference ascribed to divine being is couched in the traditional formula of "one essence, three *hypostaseis*" (*mia ousia, treis hypostaseis*).[65] It is this formula that is explicated in chapter 8 of Book One of *The Orthodox Faith*, a chapter that constitutes one of the classic discussions of the topic in the history of Christian thought.

64. Joh.D. *OF* I.8.262–65; my translation (cf. trans. Chase, 187).
65. Joh.D. *OF* I.8.23 (trans. Chase, 177).

John's exposition begins, as does the creed, with the declaration of one God:

> Therefore, we believe in one God: one principle [*mian archan*], without beginning, uncreated, indestructible and immortal, eternal, unlimited, uncircumscribed, unbounded, infinite in power, simple, uncompounded, incorporeal, unchanging, unaffected, unchangeable, inalterate, invisible, source of goodness and justice, light intellectual and inaccessable; power which no measure can give any idea of but which is measured only by His own will, for He can do all things whatsoever He pleases....[66]

At this point, John declares God's role in creating, preserving, and filling all things.[67] Then the theme of "oneness" is resumed, and John offers a string of descriptions focusing on the unity of nearly all that can be claimed for the Godhead. God is said to be:

> one substance (*mian ousian*)
> one godhead (*mian theotata*)
> one power (*mian dynamin*)
> one will (*mian thelassin*)
> one operation (*mian energeian*)
> one authority (*mian exousian*)
> one lordship (*mian kyriotata*)
> one kingdom (*mian basileian*)[68]

It is immediately after this that God is declared to be

> ... known in three perfect [or complete] Persons [*en trisi teleias hypostasesi gnoridzomenon*] and adored with one adoration [*mia proskynasai*], believed in and worshipped by every rational creature [*pasas logikas ktiseos*], united [*hanomenais*] without confusion [*asyngkutos*] and distinct without separation [*adiastatos diairoumenais*], which is beyond understanding [*paradoxon*].[69]

In the light of our theme, several considerations urge themselves upon us. For one, the claims made above about God's triunity are affirmed as ultimately incomprehensible, a point that underscores the apophatic character of theological knowledge. We need to keep this affirmation in view as a reminder that John's theology is founded on a basis not derivable from

---

66 Joh.D. *OF* I.8.1–8 (trans. Chase, 176).
67. Joh.D. *OF* I.8.11 (trans. Chase, 177).
68. Joh.D. *OF* I.8.21–23 (trans. Chase, 177).
69. Joh.D. *OF* I.8.23–26 (trans. Chase, 177).

unaided reason or the general character of creation. Even analogies that might possibly gain a certain illuminating power, when viewed retrospectively in the light of revelation, are of little interest. John is so certain that the quest for a fit analogy is basically fruitless that he barely takes it up at all. After comparing the relationship of Father and Son to that of fire and light,[70] he seemingly throws up his hands and says:

> For it is impossible to find in creation any image which exactly portrays the manner of the Holy Trinity in Itself. For that which is created is also compounded, variable, changeable, circumscribed, having shape, and corruptible; so, how shall it show with any clarity the superessential divine essence which is far removed from all such? It is evident that all creation is subject to these several conditions and that it is of its own nature subject to corruption.[71]

It might be helpful to point out here that John Damascene moves in a somewhat different mental world from that which informs Augustine's Trinitarianism. Both John and Augustine recognize the limitations of drawing on images from the created world to give fitting form to the Trinity; but Augustine is more hopeful, or at least more interested, in finding analogies that might draw one closer to the goal.[72]

The tendency of John's thought is to cling to unknowability and work out the implications of that rather than merely assert it and, in practice, try to circumvent it. This consistency reflects the depth of his commitment to the enormous gulf separating God and the world. By the eighth century, the real significance of confessing that God freely created all that is, visible and invisible, stood out with great clarity and became part of the bedrock convictions underlying the prevailing forms of theological reflection. The immutable God could only be compared to creation in ways that are ultimately more misleading than helpful. The creation, rather than reflecting its Creator, stands in stark contrast in virtually every respect: it is complex and unstable and intrinsically given to change.[73]

---

70. Joh.D. *OF* I.8.154–165 (trans. Chase, 183).

71. Joh.D. *OF* I.8.165–171 (trans. Chase, 183).

72. The crucial Book XV of *De Trinitate* indicates Augustine's quest for fitting symbols and his reservations about the adequacy of any particular symbol to give expression to the Trinity. See Burnaby's translation in his edition of *Augustine: Later Work*, 126–81.

73. This conviction, carried over into Christology, lay at the basis of Apollinarianism; see Prestige, *Fathers*, 94–119.

Another point that demands to be made is that the "one" (*mia*) used as a modifier for God and all the items in the list of ascriptions above is used univocally and carries with it the meaning of "identical" or "the very same." This contention is not necessarily self-evident: the "one" that qualifies "one God" could conceivably have a sense different from the same word used to modify "will" or "power." That each offers the meaning of "one and the same," and not something like "of equal but separate magnitude," is indicated by the presence in the list of "one substance." Here is a phrase that emerged from the fourth-century controversies with the meaning of *homoousios* (i.e., the exact same substance). In like manner, such attributes as "one will" and "one operation (or energy)" can be taken as willing and acting as one and not merely agreement. This reading is borne out by the cumulative argument of chapter 8 of Book One. Near the end of that chapter, we read:

> Accordingly, all things whatsoever the Son has from the Father the Spirit also has, including His very being. And if the Father does not exist, then neither does the Son or the Spirit; and if the Father does not have something, then neither does the Son or the Spirit. Furthermore, because of the Father, that is, because of the fact that the Father is, the Son and Spirit are; and because of the Father, the Son and the Spirit have everything that they have, that is to say, because of the fact that the Father has them, excepting the being unbegotten, the begetting, and the procession. For it is only in these personal properties that the three divine [*hypostaseis*] differ from one another, being indivisibly divided by the distinctive note of each individual [*hypostasis*] . . . By the three [*hypostaseis*] we understand that God is uncompounded and without confusion; by the consubstantiality of the [*hypostaseis*] and their existence in one another and by the indivisibility of the identity of will, operation, virtue, power, and so to speak, motion that we understand that God is one. For God and His Word and His Spirit are really one God.[74]

There is no suggestion anywhere in *The Orthodox Faith* that the individual *hypostaseis* possess separate wills or the capacity for separate action. On the contrary, will and operation (understood either as action or the capacity to act) reside in the common nature or essence and not in the *hypostaseis* individually. This point, in fact, will become crucial in the context of Christology when Trinitarian reasoning is brought to bear on the issue of whether the incarnate Son possesses one or two wills and operations. In the immediate context, the point is that the only thing that really distinguishes the three

---

74. Joh.D. *OF* I.8.195–203, 217–22 (trans. Chase, 184–85).

hypostaseis from one another is the manner of their respective origins. What binds them together, inseparably, in common substance, action, and so on, is "their existence in one another," their mutual indwelling that is summed up by the single word, *perichoresis*.

A new problem emerges at this point. The univocal use of the word "one" in the above passages might seem to suggest that, for John Damascene, the divine nature is in fact comprehensible after all. But for him, the oneness always has to be held in tension with the threeness; neither is somehow collapsible into the other. Each "number" carries its own meaning without making the irreducible mystery less mysterious. As argued earlier, John is committed to staying within the received language of sacred tradition, that is, Scripture as interpreted by the authoritative fathers. For him, that means clinging to Triunity as the highest revelation available to us ("Indeed, He has given us knowledge of Himself in accordance with our capacity . . .").[75] There is nowhere an attempt to reconcile oneness and threeness by some higher vision whereby either unity or plurality can claim to be the fundamental reality and its opposite taken as a mere way-station on the road to deeper insight.

John Damascene affirms the oneness of the divine *hypostaseis* primarily on the basis of the received tradition. But what is the larger significance of such an affirmation for his thought? To insist that the three *hypostaseis* are one in virtually every respect might in fact be a thinly disguised form of modalism. John knew this danger, of course, but insists on the basis of both Scripture and natural reasoning, that God is indeed one.[76]

That Scripture (as authoritatively interpreted) is the more important of these two is evident from John's appeal to the "unity of nature" (*physin henotatas*).[77] The latter bears testimony to God's unity in a way that might suggest that creation does reflect the being of its Creator. But creation has discordant elements at work within it, elements that suggested to other religious traditions that multiple, and perhaps conflicting, powers were present in the world. How then might the unity of nature be affirmed if not on the basis of a revelation that attributed the discordant side to the presence of evil brought on by the Fall, or God's judgment in response to that evil? John does not discuss the presence of evil in the immediate context, but his insistence on natural unity suggests strongly that he views created existence in terms of both creation and the fall into sin. It would seem that nature must,

---

75. Joh.D. *OF* I.1.17–19 (trans. Chase, 166).
76. See Joh.D. *OF* I.3.1–3; I.7.28–29; I.8.21–23 (trans. Chase, 168,175,177)
77. Joh.D. *OF* I.7.28–29 (trans. Chase, 175).

for John, be read in a certain perspective in order to receive its proper focus; one must first know the Creator before creation can be seen in its true light.

That an adequate understanding depends on a prior knowledge of the Creator is apparent in John Damascene's evaluation of the "heresies" of the Jews and the Greeks. Each, for him, had a partial grasp of the truth; each had that part of the truth that the other lacked:

> Thus, on the one hand, the unity of nature exposes the polytheistic error of the Greeks; on the other hand, the doctrine of the Word and the Spirit demolishes the teaching of the Jews. At the same time, the good in both of these heresies remains: from the Jewish opinion [*haireseos*] the unity of nature; and from Hellenism the unique distinction according to persons.[78]

The doctrine of the Trinity is not viewed as a conflation of Jewish monotheism and Hellenistic polytheism, even though a combination of the two might seem to point in that direction. What each ultimately requires, from John's perspective, is grounding in Scripture.

This latter point may not be immediately obvious. Chapters 3, 5, and 6 of Book One all offer some kind of rational basis for the Trinity.[79] Does the world reflect the being, as well as the existence, of its Creator after all?

Two points demand to be made. First of all, John qualifies his initial claim that God's existence is self-evident by including the awareness of God's majesty [*megaleion*] as well.[80] That this majesty entails unity is supported elsewhere in *The Orthodox Faith*. The logic of ultimate oneness unfolds in chapter 9 of Book One:

> The Divinity is simple [*aploun*] and uncompounded. But that which is composed of several different things is compounded [*syntheton*]. Consequently, should we say that [various attributes] are essential differences in God, then, since He is composed of so many things, He will not be simple, but compounded, which is impious [*asebeias*] to the last degree.[81]

To be "synthetic" is to have the ingredients of possible conflict or disintegration within. For John, the ultimately unknowable God cannot have

---

78. Joh.D. *OF* I.7.28–32 (trans. Chase, 175)

79. Even a cursory reading of these chapters reveals that the appeal to reason is made to those who, in many respects, have already accepted certain Christian (or at least biblical) presuppositions.

80. Joh.D. *OF* I.1.15–17 (trans. Chase, 166).

81. Joh.D. *OF* I.9.1–6 (trans. Chase, 189).

this potential because perfection is intrinsic to his definition of God.[82] The divine essence may be beyond knowing, but certain stable conclusions can nevertheless be drawn about God based on God's manifestation in both nature and history.

A second point needs to be made. Lacking a full grounding in revelation, the Jewish and Greek insights necessarily fall short of the truth. Even the Jewish view, based as much or more on the Hebrew scriptures and the experience underlying them as it is on any observations based on creation, lacks fullness because it fails to take into account certain dimensions of that very revelation. John would argue the Trinitarian case with Jews by turning to the very writings that both accept: "Should the Jew gainsay the doctrine of the Word and the Spirit, then let sacred Scripture refute him and reduce him to silence."[83]

Various proof texts are then quoted, drawn from the Psalms and Job, that John believes bolster his point that the Word and Spirit are both distinct realities that are nevertheless one with God.[84] Without retracting his claim of the indispensible revelation given by and through the Son in the Incarnation, John argues for an anticipation of the doctrine of the Trinity in the Old Testament itself, where enough light is given to make the Christian teaching worthy of acceptance.

The final failure of both "Jews" and "Greeks" is the refusal to embrace the revelation of the Son and the Spirit. "Only the Son knows the Father . . . Only the Spirit knows the thoughts of God."[85] But John's reference to partly true insights raises some intriguing possibilities. Whatever the source of those insights, whether revelation or reason, from a Christian point of view they lacked the completion of the Incarnation. John could nevertheless value them in the light of the Trinity. Incomprehensible in itself, the Trinity casts a retrospective light on the seemingly contradictory viewpoints given above and reveals how they in fact cohere. John does not press the point, but the seeds for a view of the doctrine of the Trinity as a necessary constituent for the unifying of human thought have perhaps been planted.

Some, notably Adolf Harnack, have argued that the Trinitarian conception is itself the product of the quest to resolve the tension created by conflicting views, that it is an apologetic strategy aimed at synthesizing the basic claims of primitive Christianity and the quite different vision of the

---

82. Joh.D. *OF* I.5.13–16 (trans. Chase, 172).
83. Joh.D. *OF* I.7.33–34 (trans. Chase, 176).
84. Ps 118:89; 106:20; 32:6; Job 33:4.
85. Joh.D. *OF* I.1.6–10 (trans. Chase, 165); Matt 11:27; 1 Cor. 2:11.

larger Hellenistic society into which Christianity spread.[86] This contention raises questions far beyond the scope of my study. What should be stressed here is that John clearly believes that the teachings he has received from trusted sources have an altogether different basis, a basis grounded in the coming of the Son and the bestowal of the Spirit.

That basis, however, did not exclude making use of the language of the philosophical schools. One need only glance at John's *Philosophical Chapters*, which constitute a lexicon of terms, to see how indebted John is to the broad intellectual tradition of the ancient world. His use of pagan philosophy is by no means unprecedented. Virtually every Christian thinker, from the second century onwards, made extensive use of thought forms drawn from the larger culture. The appropriation of terminology grounded in prevailing schools of thought proved both indispensible and fraught with danger. On the one hand, the need for increased precision demanded that Christian thinkers employ carefully worked-out concepts and modes of reasoning; on the other hand, extra-Christian terms often had implications that carried theological thinking in directions antithetical to essential Christian affirmations. Georges Florovsky states the problem well:

> Christian thought . . . was maturing but gradually and slowly, by a way of trial and retraction. The early Christian writers would often describe their new vision of faith in the terms of the old and current philosophy. They were not always aware of, and certainly did not always guard against, the ambiguity which was involved in such an enterprise. By using Greek categories Christians were forcing upon themselves, without knowing it, a world which was radically different from that in which they dwelt by faith. Thus they were often caught between the vision of their faith and the inadequacy of the language they were using. . . In fact, the new vision required new terms and categories for its adequate and fair expression. It was the urgent task for Christians "to coin new names," *kainotomein ta onomata*, in the phrase of St. Gregory of Nazianzus.[87]

Short of coming up with absolutely new names, the challenge of the whole patristic era was to pull and stretch existing language to accomodate insights previously unexpressed or expressed in misleading ways. Two examples of such a process are *hypostasis* and *perichoresis*, each of which had non-theological meanings that were radically altered in the course of intense

---

86. See, for instance, Harnack, *Dogma*, 4:336–39; and Harnack, *What is Christianity?*, 204–24.

87. Florovsky, "Athanasius," 41.

theological reflection and debate. The remainder of this chapter will focus on these two words.

In our introductory chapter, the Cappadocian achievement of distinguishing *hypostasis* and *ousia* from each other was cited as both a monumental turning point in ancient Christian thought and an example of terminological clarification. The distinction emerged in the midst of controversy and brought about a more adequate way of expressing realities that hitherto had been articulated in a manner almost certain to mislead.

Given the necessary limitations of all language about God, a conviction essential to John Damascene's apophaticism, one could claim that any term whatsoever is bound to be misleading—and so it will be. But the quest for greater adequacy of expression was an attempt to build up a fund of reasonably stable meanings providing the least inadequate mode of access to a reality that was finally inexpressible. In the case of the Trinity, creativity was especially called for because no term was readily available to speak of the "personal" character of God in distinction to God's "substance." the common Greek word for person, *prosopon*, carried the connotation of face or mask and could therefore take the unwary in the direction of modalism.[88] *Hypostasis* held much the same danger. In the era of Niceas and beyond, it was virtually a synonym of *ousia*, both of which were frequently used to indicate the substance or being that underlay the reality of an individual thing.[89] By separating *hypostasis* from *ousia*, the Cappadocians gave new content to an old word and, with that new content, forged new ways of expressing insights and convictions that hitherto had existed in unstable forms capable of diverse interpretations. Long before the time of John of Damascus, *hypostasis* had acquired a stable meaning, at least with regard to the Trinity. John echoes that meaning quite clearly. In his *Philosophical Chapters*, he defines *ousia* as "being in the strict sense."[90] *Hypostasis*, by contrast, can work in distinctly different ways:

> The word *hypostasis* has two meanings. Thus, when used in the strict sense it means substance simply. However, the *hypostasis* subsisting in itself means the individual and the distinct person.[91]

---

88. See Prestige's discussion in *Patristic Thought*, 157–162; and Chesnut's essay, "Two Prosopa," 392–409.

89. Note the qualification Prestige would give to this statement in *Patristic Thought*, 188–96.

90. See the Greek text in Kotter, *Schriften* 1:93 (trans. Chase, 55).

91. Kotter, *Schriften*, 1:93 (trans. Chase, 55).

Hypostasis can therefore continue to work in an early fourth-century manner but, when placed in a Trinitarian context, becomes the linguistic vehicle for conveying the irreducible distinctiveness of Father, Son, and Spirit.

But how might realities that share the same substance and act with one will be distinguished from each other? That is the fundamental question facing classical Trinitarianism. Change the terms of the traditional definition slightly and the problem "resolves" itself: either God becomes a single "person" with multiple manifestations or there are in fact several "gods," perhaps hierarchically ordered. The first of these two solutions was embodied in various forms of modalism, most notably that of Sabellius. The second enjoyed temporary success in one or another form of Arianism and resurfaced in the tritheism of the monophysite, John Philoponus.[92] John Damascene, as a champion of the Cappadocian answer, rejected both of these ways.

John framed the distinctions within divine being in terms of three distinct *hypostaseis*. In chapter 2 of Book One, he declares that God is in three *hypostaseis* (*en trisin hypostasesi*). These three "are one in all things save in the being unbegotten, the being begotten, and the procession" (*kata panta hen eisi plan tas agennasias kai tas genaseos kai tas ekporeuseos*).[93] That differences exist, we know by revelation. How they exist, what (so to speak) they look like, we cannot possibly say:

> For the Father is uncaused and unbegotten, because He is not from anything, but has His being from Himself and does not have from any other anything whatsoever that he has. Rather, He Himself is the principle [*arche*] and cause [*aitia*] by which all things naturally exist as they do. And the Son is begotten of the Father, while the Holy Spirit is Himself also of the Father—although not by begetting, but by procession. Now, we have learned there is a difference [*diaphoras*] between begetting and procession, but what the manner [*tropos*] of this difference is we have not learned at all.[94]

Once again, as one approaches the true nature of God, this time in its "personal" dimension, one is left to stand in ignorance. John recognizes the limitations under which he must work but attempts to say as much as he possibly can. What he presents in chapter 8 of Book One might be summarized as follows:

---

92. See Prestige, *Patristic Thought*, 282–83.
93. Joh.D. *OF* I.2.16–19 (trans. Chase, 167).
94. Joh.D. *OF* I.8.189–93 (trans. Chase, 184).

> *Father*: unbegotten; uncaused; begetter of Son; sender of (proceeding) Spirit; "superior to the other *hypostaseis* as their source (*arche*); equal to the others in power, glory, eternality, etc."[95]
>
> *Son*: begotten of the Father (eternally); "caused," yet in no way inferior to the Father; not begetting[96]
>
> *Spirit*: proceeding (from Father, through Son); sent out or emitted from Father (out of Father's substance); not the cause of either Father or Son[97]

What might appear as bare (and perhaps sterile) assertions devoid of significant content begin to take on developed meaning as John teases out the implications of these interrelationships. Note, in the following paragraphs, the interlocking logic of John's Trinitarian thinking, derived in part from what is resident in the names of the *hypostaseis*.

The *Father*, as Father, has no prior cause.[98] But the Father, in order to be a father, must have an offspring. That offspring is the Son. The Father is therefore in some sense superior (because ontologically prior) to the Son.[99] If the Father existed before the Son, then there was an interval in which the Father was not yet a father. If such an interval existed, then the begetting of the Son brought about some alteration of the Father, which is impossible given the immutability necessarily entailed in divine perfection.[100] The Son must therefore be co-eternal with the Father.[101]

The *Son*, as Son of the Father, does have a cause. As offspring, he is begotten, not created.[102] Since he shares the one substance of the Father, along with one will and operation, he is equal in these and every other respect except in the manner of his origin.[103] His relationship to the Father is not

---

95. Joh.D. *OF* I.8.30–33 (trans. Chase, 177).

96. Joh.D. *OF* I.8.34–50 (trans. Chase, 177–78).

97. Joh.D. *OF* I.8.172–94 (trans. Chase, 183–84).

98. Joh.D. *OF* I.8.30–31 (trans. Chase, 177). The Father is "begotten of no one" (*ouk ek tinos gennathenta*) and "alone is uncaused and unbegotten" (*anaition de kai agennaton monon hyparchonta*).

99. Joh.D. *OF* I.6.147–52 (trans. Chase, 182). "And if we say the Father is the principle [*archan*] of the Son and greater [*meizona*] than the Son, we are not giving to understand that He comes before the Son either in time or in nature . . . nor in anything save causality."

100. Joh.D. *OF* I.8.51–52 (trans. Chase, 178).

101. Joh.D. *OF* I.8.44–48 (trans. Chase, 178).

102. Joh.D. *OF* I.8.36 (trans. Chase, 177).

103. Joh.D. *OF* I.8.117–19 (trans. Chase, 181).

reversible, nor can he assume the role of Father in relation to the Spirit. That is, he is begotten, but he cannot in turn beget or cause to proceed.[104]

The *Spirit*, as that *hypostasis* which proceeds from the Father, can neither beget nor be begotten. If he were begotten, he too would be a Son.[105] Proceeding, then, is distinct from generation and gives the Spirit a unique relationship to the Father. The Spirit's relationship to the Son is also unique: unlike the Latin West, from Augustine onwards, John Damascene and the Greek tradition generally understood the Spirit as proceeding from the Father and through the Son.[106] He is communicated or imparted (*metadidomenon*) by the Son.[107] If he were to proceed from the Son (as the *filioque* clause added to the creed asserts), then he has two sources of origin and the Father is not the sole source (*monarche*) of the Godhead.[108]

The summary way in which we have presented the interrelationships of the divine *hypostaseis* in the last few pages has been a deliberate attempt to expose the bare bones of the Trinitarian structure. For John and his tradition, each *hypostasis* has a unique and irreplaceable connection with each of the other two. Whatever else can be said, the generalizations should be stressed at this point: Trinitarian "personhood" exists in a relationship of *hypostaseis*; and each *hypostasis* is stamped with uniqueness derived from the nature of its origin.

Uniqueness of origin, then, creates real and indelible differences within the Trinity. That being so, how might one go on to claim that each *hypostasis* is equal in all respects, sharing one nature, will, and operation? John Damascene illustrates the possibility of linking the two with a analogy, one of few he uses, drawn from created experience. He argues that Adam, Eve, and Seth each had an individual manner of origin (*alla toi tas hyparxeos*) and yet each shared a common nature. Both Adam and Eve were unbegotten, Adam having been formed from the ground by God and Eve having been created from Adam's rib. Only Seth was created in the now-ordinary human way. So each came into existence in a way that was different from the other two but at no sacrifice to his or her essential humanness.[109]

This analogy does just what an analogy is supposed to do. It successfully makes a limited point without needing to draw attention to the ways

---

104. Joh.D. *OF* I.8.49–51 (trans. Chase, 182). See also Joh.D. *OF* I.8.286–88 (trans. Chase, 188).

105. Joh.D. *OF* I.8.288–90 (trans. Chase, 188).

106. See Meyendorff, *Byzantine Theology*, 91–94.

107. Joh.D. *OF* I.8.289–91 (trans. Chase, 188).

108. Joh.D. *OF* I.8.30 (trans. Chase, 177).

109. Joh.D. *OF* I.8.119–22 (trans. Chase, 181).

in which it does not apply. And the point made is that difference in origin does not necessarily indicate a difference in substance. In the final section, we will take up other analogies that John uses in an attempt to illustrate how seemingly disparate realities can be combined.

Perichoresis: A Summing Up

The burden of the previous parts of our chapter was to lay out John Damascene's understanding of how God is related to the created world and within the divine nature. For John, the world can persuade us of God's existence and majesty but can do no more, apart from revelation. Revelation supplies what is missing in creation by manifesting the three-fold "personhood" of the one God who, despite internal distinctions, has one substance, will, and operation. This manifestation still does not bring us knowledge of God's essence because that lies beyond the boundary of what can be seen or known. Rather, it provides the indispensible focus for grasping what God has deemed necessary for us to know regarding the divine nature. Human language, shaped by revelation, does have value then as an access point, a threshold, offering entrance into a kind of spiritual vision that is ultimately beyond comprehension. Such, in broad terms, is the shape of John's understanding of the way in which creation, revelation, and the Trinity coordinate.

The Trinity, as presented to us in revelation as mediated through the holy tradition, is therefore a unity of being and action eternally existing in three uniquely derived subsistent *hypostaseis*. The "one" is not reducible to the "three" nor the "three" to the "one." Identity and difference exist, as it were, as two poles, each of which must be acknowledged. Orthodox believers must affirm both poles because to embrace only one is to distort the revealed character of God.

Perhaps it all could have been left there were it not for the human tendency to move toward one extreme or the other. Even the acknowledgement of paradox and mystery could not prevent minds from focusing on the instabilities inherent in current formulations. The polarity of Trinitarian belief had been spelled out, but little had been done to clarify, within the severe limits of unknowability to be sure, the nature of the connection between the two poles. The Cappadocians' solution, for all its monumental quality, did not provide a definitive way of speaking of and thinking about the relationship of the three *hypostaseis* to each other or to the common substance. Their classic formula (*mia ousia, treis hypostaseis*) sharpened the difference between the differentiated *hypostaseis* and did much to give clarity to Trinitarian "personhood" but stopped short of articulating a satisfactory way of holding the parts together. This lack is arguably evident in Gregory of Nyssa's famous *Quod non sin tre dii (That We Should Not Think of Saying There Are Three Gods)* addressed to Ablabius, in which Cyril Richardson claims to find the rudiments of *perichoresis*.[110] Gregory does argue that each of the *hypostaseis* is involved in every action of the Trinity but illustrates his point that in ways that suggest that they act in a serial fashion, that is, a fashion that throws up the image of cooperation rather than that of a common will and operation.

Our claim about Gregory is far from clear-cut. On the one hand, Gregory can assert: "The Father is God and the Son is God; and yet by the same affirmation God is one, because no distinction of nature or of operation is to be observed in the Godhead."[111] He can go on to claim:

> Although we acknowledge the nature is undifferentiated, we do not deny a distinction with respect to causality. That is the only way by which we distinguish one [*hypostasis*] from the other, by believing, that is, that one is the cause and the other depends on the cause.[112]

On the other hand, Gregory can also say:

> For the word for the operation cannot be divided among many when they mutually bring to effect a single action . . . As we have already said, the principle of the overseeing and beholding [*theatikes*] power is the unity in Father, Son, and Holy Spirit. It issues from the Father, as from a spring. It is actualized by the Son, and its grace is perfected by the power of the Holy Spirit.[113]

This is immediately qualified by these words:

> No activity is distinguished among the [*hypostaseis*], as if it were brought to completion individually by each one of them or separately apart from their joint supervision. Rather is all providence, care and direction of everything, whether in the sensible creation or of heavenly nature, one and not three. The preservation of what exists, the rectifying of what is amiss, the instruction of what is set right, is directed by the holy Trinity. But it is not divided into three parts according to the number of

---

110. See Hardy and Richardson, *Later Fathers*, 243. Note should be made of the counter-claim that *perichoresis* had no Trinitarian application until shortly before the time of John of Damascus; Prestige, *Patristic Thought*, xxxiii.

111. Greg Nyssa "On Not Three Gods" (Hardy and Richardson, *Later Fathers*, 266).

112. Ibid.

113. Ibid., 263.

[*hypostaseis*] acknowledged by the faith, so that each operation, viewed by itself, should be the work of the Father alone, or of the only-begotten by himself, or of the Holy Spirit separately.[114]

Gregory's language strains at keeping together the work of the eternally distinct *hypostaseis*, but it falls short of uniting them with the conceptuality of "mutual indwelling."

Perichoresis, as we find it used in John of Damascus, provides the clarification missing in Gregory of Nyssa.[115] Nearly four centuries separated their work. In the years separating the fourth and eighth centuries, great terminological advances emerged, especially with regard to Christology. I would argue that *perichoresis* achieved its terminological resiliency by being adapted to the new insights made possible by Chalcedon and the two or more centuries of subsequent debate generated by Chalcedon. We have noted John's use of Chalcedonian concepts, if not always the exact language, in describing how the *hypostaseis* of the Trinity are related. To say that they are united and inseparable without merging, blending, or being confused, is to move within the thought world of the Fourth Council.[116] A clearer way now existed for stating how the elements of the Trinity fit together without swallowing each other up.

Perichoresis functions then as a summing up, a condensation, of an important aspect of the doctrine of the Trinity expressed in Chalcedonian terms. The four crucial adverbs of the Chalcedonian Definition (*asyngkutos, atreptos, adiairetos, akoristos*), along with other parallel expresssions, could of themselves provide concise and cogent articulation to identity and difference within the Trinity. What *perichoresis* contributes is a further step in concision, in which the Chalcedonian conceptuality could be gathered up and uttered in a single term. That term, which we have generally rendered "mutual indwelling," is of course not self-explanatory: it requires to be funded by the classical delineations of the Trinity (and Incarnation). In light of that larger context, *perichoresis* provides increased intelligibility to the notion of union-without-absorption.

---

114. Ibid.

115. Earlier scholarship posited that John Damascene drew on an anonymous seventh-century figure who was called Pseudo-Cyril and who wrote, under the name of Cyril of Alexandria, an exposition of the Trinity that John drew on heavily. It is included in the "Dubia et Aliena" of Cyril in *MPG* 77. More recent scholarship, as found in Louth's *St John Damascene*, reverses the older view and makes John's *The Orthodox Faith* a source for Ps.-Cyril, who (according to the researches of Vassa Conticello) was really a fourteenth-century figure whom Conticello identifies at Joseph the Philosopher; see Louth, *Damascene*, 87; and Conticello, "Pseudo-Cyril's '*De Ss. Trinitate*.'"

116 Joh.D. *OF* 1.14.11–18 (trans. Chase, 202).

Can more be said? John clearly denies to the mutually indwelling *hypostaseis* any parallels from within the created realm. He is less insistent on this point when his attention turns to Christology. The assumption by the Son of a full human nature allows for analogical possibilities from which the transendent Trinity is shut off. One such analogy, drawn from Stoic physics, will be examined in the following chapter.[117]

As for the Trinity, there is a type of analogy, a sort of analogy in reverse, that John uses. Reversed analogy takes something from created existence and, if effect, turns it inside out. It roughly follows this pattern: human life is such and such; God's life is just the opposite. Such a move can go beyond saying something like we are finite and God is in-finite, although that too fits the pattern. There are instances that seem to have more overlap with human experience than simple negation does.

The Trinity provides at least some connection with our condition by virtue of its description in terms of *hypostasis* and *ousia* (or *physis*). The first term, despite the problems such a move makes, is often rendered "person." The latter terms are frequently translated "substance (or essence)" and "nature" respectively. One can note, without pressing for univocality of meaning, that each of these terms can find application in the realm of humanity. John used these "shared" terms to move in two different directions. In a marginal addition to chapter 8 of Book One, he lays out this double movement. As regards humans, he says:

> One should know that it is one thing actually to observe [*thereisthai*] something and another to see it through reason [*logoi*] and thought [*epinoi*]. Thus, in all creatures there is an actual distinction to be seen between the individual substances. Peter is seen to be actually distinct from Paul. But, that which is held in common, the connection, and the unity is seen by reason and thought. Thus, in our mind we see that Peter and Paul are of the same nature and have one common nature, for each is a mortal rational animal and each is a body animated by a rational and understanding soul. Hence, this common nature is perceived by the reason. Now, individual persons do not exist in one another at all, but each is separate and by itself, that is to say, is distinct and considered in itself, since it has a great many things to distinguish it from the other. For truly, they are separated in place and they differ in time, judgment, strength, form—or shape, habit, temperament, dignity, manner of life, and all other distinctive properties—but most of all, they differ by the fact that

---

117. The work of Sambursky on ancient physics offers links with the christological dogma that bear close study; see the bibliographical entries under his name.

they do not exist in each other but separately. Hence, we speak of two, or three, or several men.[118]

As regards the Trinity, John reverses the move he has just made with humans:

> The aforesaid is true of all creation, but is quite the contrary in the case of the holy, superessential, all-transcendent, and incomprehensible Trinity. For, here, that which is common and one is considered in actually by reason of the co-eternity and identity of substance, operation, and will, and by reason of the agreement in judgment and the identity of power, virtue, and goodness—I did not say similarity, but identity—and by reason of the one surge of motion. For there is one essence, one goodness, one virtue, one intent, one operation, one power—one and the same, not three similar to one another, but one and the same motion of the three [*hypostaseis*] . . . It is by thought that the distinction is perceived. For we know one God and Him in the properties of fatherhood, and sonship, and procession only. The difference we conceive of according to the cause and effect and the perfection of the [*hypostasis*], that is to say, His manner of existing.[119]

The reversal is clear: whereas humans are observably distinct and their commonality is discerned by reason, God is known as both one and differentiated in a contrary (*anapalin*) way. The Godhead, by its acts, presents itself as one. It is by thought (*epinoia*) that we are able to distinguish between the *hypostaseis*, whose unity would otherwise make them indistinguishable.

How then are the *hypostaseis* related to each other in their distinctiveness? John Damascene always has the twin dangers of modalism and tritheism in view as he articulates the received position. The former danger sacrifices difference; the latter breaks the unity. Each fails to see that the bond that holds oneness and difference together is "mutual indwelling." It is the reality of *perichoresis* that keeps the polarity of Trinitarian language from flying apart. *Perichoresis*, with its underlying structure embedded in the conceptuality of Chalcedon, allows John to play with seemingly contradictory statements about God and to do so with dexterity and confidence:

> For with the uncircumscribed Godhead we cannot speak of any difference in place, as we do with ourselves, because the [*hypostaseis*] exist in one another [*en allalais gar al hypostaseis eisin*], not so as to be confused, but so as to adhere closely together

---

118. Joh.D. *OF* 1.8.223–37 (trans. Chase, 185–86).
119. Joh.D. *OF* I.8.238–53 (trans. Chase, 186).

as expressed in the words of the Lord when He said: "I in the Father and the Father in me" [*Ego in toi patri, kai ho patar en emoi*]. Neither can we speak of a difference in will, or judgment, or operation, or virtue, or any other whatsoever of those things which in us give rise to a definite real distinction. For that reason, we do not call the Father and the Son and the Holy Ghost three Gods, but one God, the Holy Trinity, in whom the Son and the Holy Ghost are related to one Cause without any composition or blending such as is the coalescence of Sabellius. For they are united, as we said, so as not to be confused, but to adhere closely together, and they have their [mutual indwelling—*perichorasin*] one in another without any blending or mingling and without change or division of substance such as is the division held by Arius. Thus, one must put it concisely, the Godhead is undivided in things divided, just as in three suns joined together without any intervening interval there is one blending and the union of the light.[120]

The language of "mutual indwelling" gives cogency here to a variety of expressions that would otherwise hover on the edge of confusion. John does not dissolve the ultimate mystery of God's being but provides a way of approaching it that appears to be faithful to the demands of sacred tradition.

Seemingly less cogent is John Damascene's claim that divine unity is evident in a manner parallel to that of human plurality. Both, he argues, are givens from which their opposites must be deduced by thought (*epinoia*). But neither "oneness" nor "threeness" in divine being has the kind of transparent self-evidence of the unity and multiplicity found in humans and other creatures. John's general intent, however, is clear: he wants to hold on the both sides of the Trinitarian equation, but he realizes one side is less problematical than the other; oneness is easier to grasp that threeness, just as Peter and Paul a separate beings are easier to comprehend than is their common humanity. Three and one, finally, hold together by having a common "place" (*topikan*), which is their "mutual indwelling."

Perichoresis or mutual indwelling embraces, then, the uniting of the one *ousia* with the three *hypostaseis* without confusion, blending, mingling, composition, change, or division of subsance. That term takes on other, though by no means distinctly different, meanings when taken out of a strictly Trinitarian context; but, with reference to the nature of God, it represents a short-hand way of focusing and summing up an understanding of the Trinity that is fundamentally Cappadocian but that has been further refined by being creatively restated in terms drawn from Chalcedonian

120. Joh.D. *OF* I.8.253–67 (trans. Chase, 186–87).

Christology. That understanding distinguishes God from the created world because mutual indwelling is without parallel in the ways humans are connected with each other; apart from the Son's revelation of the Father and the Spirit, no knowledge of God's inner life could be known. With regard to that inner life, *perichoresis* provides a way of grasping, even if on a very limited scale, how three might be one and how both variety and unity can characterize the same divine reality.

3
Perichoresis and Christ

IN CHAPTER 5 OF BOOK THREE OF JOHN DAMASCENE'S *THE ORTHODOX Faith*, we find the following passage:

> Now, as the three [*hypostaseis*] of the Holy Trinity are united without confusion and are distinct without separation and have number without the number causing division, or separation, or estrangement, or severance among them—for we recognize that the Father and the Son and Holy Ghost are one God—so the same way the natures [*physeis*] of Christ, although united, are united without confusion, and, although mutually immanent [*perichorousin*], do not suffer any change or transformation of the one into the other.[1]

The Chalcedonian link argued for in our last chapter, whereby John couches the mutually indwelling *hypostasteis* of the Trinity in the conceptuality generated by the Christology of Chalcedon, finds clear articulation here as the two doctrines are juxtaposed in essentially the same terms.

The term that marks out the peculiar character of the union lying at the heart of each doctrine, a union without absorption, is *perichoresis* in one or another of its variant forms. John uses the language of mutual indwelling or mutual immanence to bring the identity and difference entailed in both dogmas within the range of at least limited comprehensibility.

The present chapter will explore the range of that comprehensibility in relation to John's doctrine of Christ. Because nearly three hundred years of continuing christological debate stand between John and Chalcedon, it will be necessary to note certain landmarks of doctrinal advance and clarification leading up to the eighth century. Even a summary account can serve two useful purposes: it can bring into view a crucial stretch of doctrinal

---

1. Joh.D. *OF* III.5.21–29 (trans. Chase, 278).

history that is frequently neglected by those seeking some knowledge of patristic Christology; and it will indicate the interpretive angle from which I approach John's presentation.

After offering a cursory description of key moments in terminological and conceptual development, I will then lay out John's christological use of *perichoresis* as presented primarily in Book Three of *The Orthodox Faith*. My strategy will be to discuss the issue in relation to the central categories of late patristic Christology. What might be termed, in the light of later ecclesiastical history, as the Chalcedonian mainstream presented Christ in terms of two natures, human and divine, embodied in one person. That person, the Logos incarnate, possessed both a human and a divine will and both human and divine operations. These categories will be fleshed out not only in connection with Book Three but also with the help of the terminological lexicon that makes up the *Philosophical Chapters* (the *Dialectica*) and the catalogue of aberrant opinion found in *On Heresies* (*Liber de Haeresibus*).[2] These latter works, as was noted in our first chapter, actually precede *The Orthodox Faith* in the trilogy that comprises *The Fount of Knowledge* and, therefore, function as a sort of preface to John's doctrinal exposition. As such, they will be used to illuminate the expository sections; but controlling weight will be given to *The Orthodox Faith* because it is there that key terms receive their fullest and most concrete grounding.

Chalcedon and After: A Brief Sketch

The character of christological development in the three hundred years following the Council of Chalcedon (451) should be familiar enough not to require any rehearsal here. But a common tendency, noted in our first chapter, is to view Chalcedon as a conclusion, even if a very unsatisfactory one, and to regard the later controversies as so much wool-gathering or mere rehashing of earlier views. Even a standard text on patristic theology, J. N. D. Kelly's *Early Christian Doctrines*, can entitle its chapter on Chalcedon, "The Christological Settlement," and end that chapter with a few terse words about the aftermath.[3] The student might well conclude that there is no point in looking further. The following paragraphs attempt, therefore, to rectify the imbalance a bit by drawing attention to what I believe to be genuine advances.

---

2. Splendid modern editions of the Greek text of each can be found in Kotter, *Die Schriften*, vols. 1 and 4.

3. See Kelly, *Early Christian Doctrines*, 310–43.

Of the three major ecumenical councils that followed Chalcedon, at least two (Constantinople 553, Constantinople 680/681) were convened to deal with christological issues. The third (Nicea 787), with its focus on iconoclasm, clearly had christological import as well, as John's famous defense of icons made plain decades earlier.[4] The councils themselves and the intervening years saw intense debate, resulting in various kinds of gain and loss.[5]

The major loss was the final splitting of the monophysite followers of Cyril of Alexandria from those who believed Chalcedon was compatible with Cyril's teachings. At issue was Cyril's affirmation of "the one nature of the incarnate Word." While both sides could acknowledge that Christ's "nature" was in some sense composite, Chalcedonian dyophysites wanted to affirm two distinct, though inseparable, natures "after the union."[6] For monophysites, such an affirmation had Nestorian overtones. They preferred to speak of two natures "before the union" and one nature, variously understood by different monophysite factions, in the Incarnation. For Chalcedonians, this latter move appeared to entail the absorption of the human nature in the divine.

In the ensuing years, various attempts to resolve the divisions were made. None of these brought the two major parties together, but some of the contestants put forward creative solutions that became embedded in classical conciliar statements and were regarded, by the dominant party, as genuine steps forward in the process of clarification.

One such step was provided by Leontius of Byzantium (early sixth century) whose understanding of *enhypostasia* provided a way around the

4. The fundamentally christological character of the Seventh Council (787), whose ostensible focus was on the legitimacy of icons, is argued for by Kallistos Ware in Cunliffe-Jones, ed., *History of Christian Doctrine*, 191–200; Pelikan in *Christian Tradition* 2:91–145; and Meyendorff, *Byzantine Theology*, 42–53; and *Christ*, 173–82. See also Azhoul, "Perichoresis," 67–85.

5. In addition to the works by Meyendorff, Chesnut, Frend, and Harnack referred to in the first chapter (see notes 4 and 5), see the standard treatment by Sellers, *Chalcedon*, 302–50.

6. Cyril's "Second Letter to Successus" is important in this context. Advocates of both one and two natures later appealed to the authority of Cyril for their support. But even though he clung to the language of "one nature of the incarnate Word," he clearly had a *composite* nature in view: "If we speak of the only-begotten Son of God, incarnate and made man, as one, this produces no mixture . . . The nature of the Word has not passed into the nature of the flesh, or has that of the flesh into that of the Word. Rather, it is with each nature retaining its own distinctive character, being perceived as such, that the ineffable and inconceivable union of the Word which we have just described discloses to us one nature of the Son—though, as we have said, one incarnate nature." See the full text in Wiles and Santer, *Documents*, 66–71, esp. 68.

Nestorian implications monophysites believed were at the heart of the Chalcedonian Definition. In recent years, David Evans has argued that Leontius was fundamentally an Origenist in his Christology (a point to be challenged by Brian Daley) and therefore heterodox in terms of the dominant viewpoint; but his grasp of the interrelationship of Christ's two natures won widespread support, even from those who might have found his Origenism unacceptable.[7] He maintained that, while each nature remained distinct and each had all the properties "natural" to it, only the divine nature had its own *hypostasis*. Despite that, Leontius did not view the human nature as an impersonal abstraction. Its "personality" derived from the incarnate Logos who, as the one Christ, hypostatically united two natures in his one person.[8] In other words, the personality of the Logos was what gave personal expression to both of the natures. The human nature was, therefore, enabled to be "personal" without having its own separate person.

Another step toward clarification came from Leontius of Jerusalem, a contemporary of Leontius of Byzantium with whom he is frequently confused.[9] Whereas his namesake had identified the one *hypostasis*, not with the Logos but with the Christ who came into being when the Logos united with an unfallen mind in the Incarnation. Leontius of Jerusalem claimed that the pre-incarnate Logos became the center of being, holding human and divine together. It was the Logos, thus understood, who, because the human nature belonging to Christ was his human nature, could be said (in a fashion echoing Cyril) to have suffered in the flesh. This "theopaschism" became normative for the dominant group through its acceptance at the Fifth Council in 553. That council tried, without success, to conciliate the monophysites. In addition to declaring the Logos (in his human nature) the subject of the passion, it condemned the Antiochene "Three Chapters." The attempt to win over the "one nature" groups failed, but a Cyrillian reading of Chalcedon finally prevailed and the strict dyophysitism, earlier advocated by Theodoret and others, fell by the wayside.[10]

Both Leontius of Byzantium and Leontius of Jerusalem provided ways of holding to the two-nature language of Chalcedon without slipping into the Logos-anthropos schema that dogged most Antiochene attempts to articulate the character of the Incarnation. Leontius of Byzantium held the

---

7. See Evans, *Leontius,* especially chap. 4 (on Leontius and Evagrius), 84–131; and Florovsky, *Byzantine Fathers,* 191–203.

8. See Meyendorff, *Christ,* 61–63, 73–74. See also Florovsky, *Byzantine Fathers,* 198.

9. See Meyendorff, *Christ,* 61, 73.

10. Meyendorff, *Byzantine Fathers,* 29–44.

two-natures together in one person by arguing that the latter is the subject of both natures. Leontius of Jerusalem provided a way of speaking of the suffering of the impassible Logos by emphasizing that the nature that suffered was indeed that of the Logos, even though what it experienced could not touch his divine nature.

I would see three other crucial steps toward giving Chalcedon the kind of clarity and intelligibility it required to satisfy at least most of those searching for a settlement to the christological debate.

First, note should be made of the eventually emphatic distinction that most made between nature (*physis*) and person (*hypostasis*). Cyril, in an earlier period, often used the two interchangeably even though various documents show him to have been increasingly aware of crucial distinctions.[11] Both Nestorians and monophysites tended to do the same with predictable results. Nestorians, eager to preserve the impassibility of the Logos and to give point to the moral effort of the human nature, saw in the two natures two "persons" (*prosopa*).[12] Monophysites, concerned to bring all that was human and in need of redemption into the sphere of divinity, saw in Cyril's "one nature" the whole of the divine-human person. The two Leontiuses, along with others, were able to hold most of the concerns of both groups within the circle of Chalcedonian language (a) by preserving the impassible nature without apparently diminishing the humanity and (b) by making human experience (apart from sin) inseparably part of the incarnate Logos.

To distinguish *physis* and *hypostasis* in clarifying ways was, in a very real sense, a move comparable to the Cappadocian clarification of the same terms in relation to the Trinity. In both cases, when the contrast was finally and emphatically drawn, several persistent problems began to fall into place. The next step illustrates this.

Our next crucial move is the advance provided by Maximus the Confessor (c. 580–662) and others through their assertion of two wills and two operations in the incarnate Logos.[13] Many have noted a pendulum swing from council to council: claims for the unity of Christ's person seem to alternate with those maintaining the distinction of the natures. The dominant accent of Chalcedon (451) was placed on the two natures, human and divine, each preserving its own character. The next council (Constantinople

---

11. His "Second Letter to Seccensus" (quoted in part in note six above) illustrates his capacity to make such a distinction.

12. See Wand, *Four Great Heresies*, 98. The two *prosopa* united to form a single *prosopon*, but the linkage was such as to preserve the divine side of the equation from hypostatic connection with the human side. A fine analysis of Nestorius's understanding of *prosopa* can be found in Chesnut's "Two *Prosopa*," 392–409.

13. See Meyendorff, *Christ*, 131–51.

553), reacting to the "Nestorian" interpreters of Chalcedon and hoping to conciliate the monophysites, placed major emphasis on the *hypostasis*, who (as incarnate) both suffered and remained impassible.[14] Further efforts to bring the affirmers of one nature back into the fold either put forth claims that the Logos in his two natures nevertheless had only one will and one operation or ruled as off limits any discussion about the number of wills and energies.[15]

Maximus and, later, the majority at the sixth council (Constantinople 680/681) moved the pendulum back in the other direction by proclaiming that the one Christ nevertheless had two wills and two energies or operations. A Trinitarian rationale undergirded the argument. Classical Trinitarianism affirmed, along with three *hypostaseis* in one *ousia*, the absolute oneness of will and action of the entire Trinity. The locus of that oneness was the common "essence" (*ousia*) or "nature" (*physis*).

By locating will and operation in the common nature and not in the individual *hypostaseis*, the prevailing doctrine of the Trinity opened up a way for a solution to a christological problem. Both doctrines shared a common vocabulary with enough commonality of meaning to make movement back and forth between the two plausible.

What the unity of will and operation in the common essence of the Trinity offered the christological debate is this. By insisting that the *hypostaseis* of the Godhead could not be independent centers of activity, the Cappadocians and their followers had prevented understandings of divinity that would violate the essential unity of God. The "persons" of the Trinity had their own inviolable identity, but they could not act individually. Whatever, therefore, the individualizing characteristics of each *hypostasis* might be, they did not include an individual will or an independent center of operation.

This Trinitarian logic became the basis for crucial christological decisions. The position that prevailed in the Byzantine church argued that the natures hypostatically united in the incarnate Christ likewise possessed volition and activity just as the one nature of the Godhead did. In fact, one of those two natures was identical with the divine nature in its expression as Logos. Orthodox opinion, therefore, regarded will and operation as "natural" (i.e. belong to the natures) and not "personal" (i.e., belonging to the *hypostasis/hypostaseis*). If such were personal, and not natural, the full

---

14. Both Meyendorff, *Byzantine Theology*, 151; and Ware, in Cunliffe-Jones, ed., *History of Christian Doctrine*, 188–89, make this point.

15. Ware, in Cunliffe-Jones, ed., *History of Christian Doctrine*, 187–88; and Florovsky, *Byzantine Fathers*, 204–7.

humanity required by the logic of salvation would entail the presence of another "person."

Given the Trinitarian rationale, the Logos therefore needed to be the sole subject of both human and divine activity. Another "person" would have broken the hypostatic union and collapsed the notions of nature and person into one another. By locating willing and doing in the natures and not in the person, seventh-century thinkers put the duality of natures on more solid footing. They did so without sacrificing the unity of the person. In the process, a firmer line was drawn against both Nestorians and monophysites. The latter group, of course, had no place for multiple wills. But the former, curiously, came out roughly in the same place by insisting that the two subjects held together in prosopic union likewise acted as one in a union of will and action.[16]

Against both the major dissenting groups, then, Maximus and, later, the sixth council urged that will and operation were intrinsic to a real human nature, even one hypostatically united to the Logos.[17] This perspective became foundational for John of Damascus a few generations later and grounded both his Christology and soteriology.

The final crucial step toward greater conceptual clarity for those working within the framework of Chalcedon was that of *perichoresis*, the theme of our study. Our last chapter argued that *perichoresis*, in relation to the Trinity, summed up and gave condensed expression to a centuries-long development that integrated insights drawn from Chalcedonian Christology with those of Cappadocian theology. The present chapter will argue that *perichoresis* in relation to the Incarnation performs a similar summing-up function in which the language of mutual indwelling gathers up the several notions presented in this section: *enhypostasia*; Logos as *hypostasis*; Logos as suffering in its human nature; nature and person as distinct; and two wills and operations. All of these intellectual moves pushed the central party toward greater integrity in its ongoing affirmation of Chalcedon's two natures in one person. We will now explore, in depth, the role *perichoresis* plays in John's exposition of this development.

Perichoresis in John Damascene's Christology

The passage from chapter 5 of Book Three of *The Orthodox Faith* that opened our present chapter made an explicit connection between the character of mutual indwelling in the Trinity and the indwelling of the two natures in the

---

16. See Florovsky, *Byzantine Fathers Century*, 207–8, 247.
17. See Meyendorff, *Christ*, 29–46.

one Christ. I referred to that connection as the Chalcedonian link. That link allows both identity and difference to be affirmed in each case: the distinct realities encompassed by each doctrine hold together in inseparable union without losing their distinctive properties.

Identity and difference, the two terms highlighted in our introductory chapter, lie at the base of *perichoresis* in every passage in which we have found it so far. I will continue to argue, throughout the rest of our study, that that pair form part of the essential skeletal structure of *perichoresis* in whatever context John might use it. True, identity and difference by themselves exhibit *perichoresis* in its most abstract form, leaving out all that makes it vital and dynamic; but they provide a kind of schematic simplicity, a scaffolding as it were, by which richer meaning can be built up.

We can begin that constructive process by examining another passage, found in chapter 7 of Book Three:

> One must know . . . that, although we say that the natures of the Lord are mutually immanent [*perichorein*], we know that this immanence [*perichoresis*] comes from the divine nature [*theias physeos*]. For this last pervades [*dia . . . diakei*] all things and indwells [*perichorei*] as it wishes, but nothing pervades it. And it communicates [*metadosi*] its own splendors to the body while remaining impassible [*apathas*] and having no part in the affections [*pathon ametochos*] of the body. For, if the sun communicates its own operations [*energeion*] to us, yet has no part in our own, then how much more so the Creator of the sun who is the Lord?[18]

In this passage, we can witness *perichoresis* taking on density of meaning and its peculiar christological connotations beginning to emerge. As with the passage quoted at the beginning of our second chapter, we will now venture some preliminary analysis as a way of focusing the discussion of the rest of the present chapter.

First of all, the passage above emphasizes the divine nature as the source and controlling center of the mutual indwelling. The bond here that holds human and divine natures together is not some third force separated from one or both of the constituents; neither is it simply a combination of the two. Rather, it arises from the divine initiative ("as it wishes"—*kathos bouletai*) and illustrates what Ketje Rozemond (following the lead of Georges Florovsky) calls "*christologie asymetrique.*"[19]

18. Joh.D. *OF* III.7,57–63 (trans. Chase, 284).

19. See Rozemond, *Christologie*, especially chap. 2 ("Christogie Asymetrique") and chap. 3 ("Christogie de la Tradition"), 17–63. See also Florovsky, "Christological Dogma," in Fries and Gros, eds., *Christ in East and West*, 45–47.

Even though John Damascene's Christology, here and elsewhere, affirms two real natures, each fully that which it represents, they are not equally active in the union. If they were, then perhaps some form of Nestorianism would be the reasonable outcome. On the other hand, if one of the natures were so dominant as to reduce the other to quiescence, then the result would not be asymmetry but the virtual reduction of the incarnate Logos to one nature. Some, of course, believe that is exactly what did happen in post-Chalcedonian Christology: Harnack, for instance, speaks of the triumph of Apollinarianism and of the crypto-monophysite character of later Greek Christian thought.[20] More light on this matter will be shed when we turn to the problem of two wills and two operations. Here, we simply note that the meaning of *perichoresis* for John must be qualified in a way that allows for the priority of the divine component.

A second point demands our attention. In the passage above, the divine nature not only has a certain kind of relationship to its own human nature but also is related to the rest of creation in a way that might be termed as mutually immanent. It is said to "pervade all things" and "indwell" according to its own choosing, all the while remaining unaffected by that which it pervades or indwells. It is not clear from the present passage whether pervading and indwelling are precisely the same, because the former embraces "all" (*panton*) while the "as it wishes" of the latter might imply selectivity. At the very least, we can say that God's relationship to creation is, in some way, analogous to the Logos's relationship to his own humanity. Whether that analogy suggests something approaching identity will be broached in our chapter on salvation.

A third point, already noted in the last paragraph, is that the divine nature remains unaffected by its relationship to its own body. The image of the sun, shining on all, affecting all, but remaining unchanged for all that, is seemingly a more fitting illustration of God's connection with creation than it is of the Incarnation. Is there no reciprocity between the two natures? We have, so far, not adduced enough textual evidence to answer the question one way or the other. At this point, however, some preliminary remarks are in order. For one, if there is no reciprocity, then perhaps John really embraces some form of monophysitism. Or perhaps the impassible character of the divine nature is "protected" by the activity of an "assumed" person, in which case mutual indwelling is really something more like prophetic inspiration. How John actually regards the mutuality of the hypostatically united natures must emerge from a close examination of his full presentation of Christology.

20. See Harnack, *Dogma*, 4:264–65.

The Scope of Book Three

Book Three of *The Orthodox Faith* focuses on the Person of Christ just as Book One concentrates on the doctrine of God as Trinity. Unlike the first book, however, the third has twice as many chapters. The Latin division of John Damascene's Exposition attempted to keep chapters of related theme together and was, therefore, more than an effort to break down the text into four equal segments. Even at that, Books Two and Four have approximately the same number of chapters as Book Three, so only Book One stands out as somewhat disproportionate.

Book Three follows a pattern somewhat parallel to the history of christological debate from Chalcedon onwards. After a preliminary statement in the first chapter about the human dilemma and the need for redemption and, therefore, the Incarnation, several sections (chapters 2 through 13) deal with problems associated with the two natures of Christ in relation to the composite *hypostasis* of the incarnate Word. Within this group, one can find discussions of the "Thrice-Holy Hymn" and the Mother of God/ *Theotokos*, which respectively concern themselves with the relation of suffering to the impassible divine nature and the issue of who is the true subject of Christ's human nature.

After this group come two chapters that are central both in location and length: chapter 14 has an extended treatment of Christ's will; chapter 15 gives equally extended handling of Christ's energies or operations.

The remaining fourteen chapters probe in greater depth the matters broached in the first half of Book Three. Chapter 16 returns to the problem of the natures. Seventeen and eighteen enlarge on the inherited teaching about the wills. Chapter 19 brings wills and operations into unity with an important exposition of "theandric operations." Chapters 20 through 25 delve into the implications of Christ's real or apparent limitations as a human capable of displaying hunger, thirst, anger, ignorance of times and locations, and so on. The final four chapters, 26 through 29, focus on the connection of the passable and the impassable in the one person of the Logos.

As with Book One, the aim of what follows will be to lay hold of the underlying logic that orders the various christological assertions that John affirms which he inherited from the dominant viewpoint stemming from Chalcedon. All the while, we will be asking our dual question: how does all this illuminate the character of *perichoresis* and how does *perichoresis*, in turn, cast light on John's presentation of Christology?

The discussion will be structured by three key themes: the two natures in the composite person of the Word; the two wills entailed in the two natures; and the two energies or operations concomitant with the two wills.

Each of these will draw into itself some related issues that will function as sub-themes within one or another of the three areas.

The Two Natures in the One Person of Christ

The bone of contention for those who dissented from Chalcedon was that the "two nature" language promulgated by the council seemed to imply something different from the "one (composite) nature" favored by Cyril and affirmed by several of the parties with perhaps divergent interpretations. A stumbling block for monophysites was the council's confirmation of Pope Leo's subsequently famous *Tome*, which, when set side by side with the Chalcedonian Declaration, seemed to encourage giving a Nestorian reading to the latter. The offending tendency of the *Tome*, according to its detractors, was that it rather neatly divided Christ's activities into two distinct categories, human and divine. The following indicates how the division would work:

> To hunger, to thirst, to be weary, and to sleep is evidently human. But to feed five thousand . . . with five loaves, and to bestow on the woman of Samaria that living water, to drink of which can secure one from thirsting again; to walk on the surface of the sea with feet that sink not, and by rebuking the storm to bring down the "uplifted waves," is unquestionably divine.[21]

Leo goes on, in the same tract, to assert that "in the Lord Jesus Christ there is one Person of God and man" and "to confess that the one Son of God is both Word and flesh."[22] But this language did not satisfy those for whom two distinct natures implied two distinct persons and who therefore regarded claims from certain quarters of "one Son of God" as merely a manner of speaking, a legal fiction as it were, referring to two separate subjects as if they were in fact one.

What was lacking, at least in the latter half of the fifth century, was some extra-Chalcedonian rationale whereby one subject could plausibly be in possession of two natures. By John Damascene's time, that rationale had long since emerged and was available for him to put into systematic order. To refer to John as a Chalcedonian then is in fact to place him within a Chalcedonian tradition that extended through the fifth and sixth ecumenical councils and the conceptual breakthroughs brilliantly wrought by such thinkers as Leontius of Byzantium, Leontius of Jerusalem, and Maximus the

---

21. The *Tome* of Leo I in Hardy and Richardson, *Later Fathers*, 365.
22. Leo, *Tome*, 366, 367.

Confessor. We allude to that history, once again, in order to locate John at the end of that developmental sequence. He may have contributed little that was truly original, but his ordering and summing up gave their thoughts historically influential form. Perhaps no clearer exposition of so-called neo-Chalcedonianism is available than *The Orthodox Faith*.

Essential to the neo-Chalcedonian position is the distinction between *physis* and *hypostasis*.[23] As we noted earlier, apart from such a distinction, some form of either Nestorianism or monophysitism is almost inevitable. These extreme tendencies, in opposite ways, break down the polarity of identity and difference, that polarity that provides the minimal basis for *perichoresis*. That there were probably many who leaned one way or the other without actually fracturing that base is doubtless true and a reminder that many, then as well as now, often tolerate a high degree of terminological vagueness and avoid the logical implications of their own stated positions. But for John and for the Fathers who preceded him, clarity and precision were not mere scholars' games; they served the truth and aided spiritual health.

What then is a *physis*? What then is a *hypostasis*? Before looking at concrete instances of these terms in John's doctrinal exposition, we can profitably examine them through the explicit definitions provided in the *Philosophical Chapters*.

As regards *physis* or "nature," we find the following:

> The nature [*physis*] of each being is the principle [*arche*] of its motion and repose . . . Now, the principles and cause of its motion and repose—or that according to which it is of its nature thus moved and rests substantially, that is to say, naturally [*physikos*] and not accidentally [*kata symbebakos*]—is called *physis*, or nature, from its *pephykenai*, or naturally having being and existing in such a manner. This is nothing other than substance [*ousia*], because it is from its substance that it has such a potentiality [*dynamin*], that is to say, of motion and repose. Now, *physis*, or nature, is so called from its *pephykenai*, or naturally having being.[24]

This definition indicates that *physis* points to a differentiated form of being in which a particular reality manifests the possibilities inherent in its type. As such, it displays the character of "substance" (*ousia*) generally. In the preceding entry in the *Philosophical Chapters*, John defines *ousia*:

---

23. See the reference to *physis* in Meyendorff, *Christ*, esp. 21–22, 28–29, 41–43, 72–73.

24. Joh.D., *Dialectica* [*Peri physeos*] 1–11 (trans. Chase, 65).

> Substance is a thing which subsists in itself and has no need of another for its existence. And again: substance is everything that subsists in itself and does not have its existence in another—that is to say, that which is not because of any other, nor has its existence in another, nor has any need of another to subsist, but which is in itself and is that in which the accident has its existence.[25]

Earlier, in chapter 30 of the *Philosophical Chapters*, John had sharpened the difference between *ousia* and *physis* by affirming a distinction drawn from pagan philosophy:

> In this ... way the pagan philosophers stated the difference between *ousia*, or substance, and *physis*, or nature, by saying that substance was being in the strict sense, whereas nature was substance which had been made specific by essential differences so as to have, in addition to being in the strict sense, being in such a way, whether rational or irrational, mortal or immortal. In other words, we may say that ... nature is that unchangeable and immutable principle and cause which has been implanted by the Creator in each species for its activities ... in men, for thinking, reasoning, and for communicating their innermost thoughts to one another through the medium of speech ....[26]

Nature, then, is that form of substance embodied in a particular species and gives that species the traits associated with it. It is crucial to underscore the fact that species, and not individuals within species, are the principal focus here.

As for individual instances of any particular species, John Damascene follows the Fathers in designating such as *hypostaseis*:

> And so the more particular they [the Fathers] called *hypostasis*, and the more general, which contained the *hypostaseis*, they called nature, but existence in the strict sense they called *ousia*, or substance.[27]

There is, therefore, a narrowing of range as one moves from being, the most general category, through nature, as the category marking off the peculiar character of a specific species, to *hypostaseis* or person (better: individual), as the term for specifying a particular manifestation of some species.

---

25 Joh.D. *Dialectica* [*Peri ousias*] 1–6 (trans. Chase, 64).

26. Joh.D. *Dialectica* [*Peri ousias*] 1–12 (trans. Chase, 55).

27. Joh.D. *Dialectica* [*Peri ousias*] 19–22. (trans. Chase, 56).

There is a common nature, then, a nature with its own "natural" traits, that runs through a species. An individual within that species may have "accidental" traits that underscore its individuality, but it will, at the same time, embody characteristics common to the species as a whole.

These preliminary definitions view *physis* and *hypostasis* in the most general sense and do little to indicate the specific character of these terms in relation to humanity and divinity. The *Philosophical Chapters* as a whole give only minor indications of the theological applications to which the concepts surveyed will be put. To find the expressly christological character of *physis* and *hypostasis*, we must turn directly to Book Three of *The Orthodox Faith*.

The Reality of the Human and the Priority of the Divine

John Damascene's presentation of the Incarnation is insistent at the outset on two claims: Christ's human nature is real and complete; and the person of the united humanity and divinity is God and not a human or a combined God-human. Both claims are made in connection with the Virgin Mary. Her assent to Gabriel's promise is foundational to what follows:

> And so, after the holy Virgin had given her assent, the Holy Ghost came upon her according to the Lord's word, which the angel had spoken, and purified her both to receive the deity of the Word and to beget.[28]

Then John makes a most interesting assertion that the Logos shaped his own humanity, a humanity that had the "natural" attributes of body and (rational, intellectual) soul:

> Then the subsistent Wisdom and Power of the Most High, the Son of God, the Consubstantial with the Father, overshadowed her like a divine seed and from her most chaste and pure blood compacted for Himself a body animated by a rational and intellectual soul as first fruits of our clay.[29]

That this animated body was not a self-standing person somehow linked with the Logos is made plain in the same passage:

> This was not by seed, but by creation through the Holy Ghost, with the form not being put together bit by bit, but being completed all at once with the Word of God Himself serving as the person of the flesh. For the divine Word was not united to an

---

28 Joh.D. *OF* III.2.16–19 (trans. Chase, 270).

29. Joh.D. *OF* III.2.19–23 (trans. Chase, 270).

already self-subsistent flesh, but, without being circumscribed, came in his own person to dwell in the womb of the holy Virgin and from the chaste blood of the ever-virgin made flesh subsist animated by a rational and intellectual soul. Taking to himself the first-fruits of the human clay, the very Word became person to the body. Thus, there was a body which was at once the body of God the Word and an animate, rational, intellectual body. Therefore, we do not say that man became God, but that God became man. For, while He was by nature perfect God, the same became by nature perfect man.[30]

That this humanity was neither illusory nor swallowed up by the divinity is underscored by the remainder of the passage we are quoting:

[The Logos] did not change His nature and neither did He just appear to be man. On the contrary, without confusion [*asynkutos*] or alteration [*analloiotos*] or division [*adiairetos*] He became hypostatically united [*henotheis kath' hypostasin*] to the rationally and intellectually animated flesh which He had from the holy Virgin and which had its existence in Him. He did not transform the nature of His divinity [*ma metalabon tan tas theototos auto physin*] into the substance of His flesh [*eis tan tas sarkos ousian*] nor the substance of His flesh into the nature of of His divinity, and neither did He effect one compound nature [*mia physin . . . syntheton*] out of His divine nature and the human nature which He assumed.[31]

Throughout these passages, John keeps in view the dual problem of Nestorianism and monophysitism. To grant the human nature a *hypostasis* other than the Logos would be a move toward the former heresy; to make the *hypostasis* of the incarnate Logos equivalent to the (single) *physis* proclaimed by other heretics would introduce alteration or confusion into the humanity of Christ.

John Damascene's complaint against Nestorians is that they split the humanity of the Logos from the divinity and make each self-standing. Further, they divide the actions of Christ into two sharply differentiated categories:

And the more humble of the Lord's actions during His sojourn among us they attribute to His humanity alone, whereas the more noble and those befitting the divinity they ascribe to God

---

30. Joh.D. *OF* III.2.23–35 (trans. Chase, 270).
31. Joh.D. *OF* III.2.35–42 (trans. Chase, 270–71).

> the Word alone. But they do not attribute the both to the same Person.³²

That not all whom John might call Nestorian would accept the above characterization does not detract from the importance of identifying the underlying assumptions at work in crucial passages in *The Orthodox Faith*.

The same might be said for John's view of monophysitism. Clearly, by the eighth century, monophysitism posed a problem, both theological and ecclesiastical, that had greater force than did the much diminished Nestorians. John devotes far more attention to it, in both *On Heresies* and *The Orthodox Faith*.³³ In the former work, we find the following description;

> The Eutychians . . . say that our Lord Jesus Christ did not take His flesh from the blessed Virgin Mary, but contend that He became incarnate in a more divine manner, For they could not conceive how God the Word could unite to Himself from the Virgin Mary this man, who was subject to the sin of his first father Adam . . .³⁴

John identifies, in the following way, those successors of Eutyches to whom the term monophysite is usually attached:

> Because of their strong attachment to Dioscorus of Alexandria, who was deposed by the Council of Chalcedon for defending the teachings of Eutyches, they opposed this council and to the limit of their ability fabricated innumerable charges against it, which charges we have . . . sufficiently refuted by showing them to be clumsy and stupid.³⁵

Along with Theodosius of Alexandria and Jacob of Syria, John singles out Severus ("the seducer from Antioch") and the John Philoponus (referred to here as John the Tritheite) for special opprobrium. The last two challenged John's understanding of the truth in the following way:

> Both of these last denied the mystery of salvation. They wrote many things against the inspired council of the 630 Fathers of Chalcedon, and they set many snares, so to speak, and "laid stumbling blocks by the wayside" for those who are lost in their

---

32. Joh.D., *Haer.* [*Nestorianoi*] 2–6 (trans. Chase, 138).

33. In *On Heresies*, Nestorianism receives six lines in the Kotter edition, while monophysitism has 213 lines; *De Schriften*, 2:48–51. See Chase, *Writings*, 138–48.

34. Joh.D., *Haer.* [*Eutychianistai*] 1–5 (trans. Chase, 138).

35. Joh.D., *Haer.* [*Aigyptiakoi . . . monophysitai*] 6–10 (trans. Chase, 138–39).

pernicious heresy. Although they hold individual substances, they destroy the mystery of the Incarnation.[36]

A few lines beyond this point, John Damascene's own words break off, and he, so to speak, allows John Philoponus to make his own case by quoting a long extract from one of the Tritheite's principal works.

The argument of John Philoponus is closely reasoned and worthy of careful study but must be given condensed treatment here. Underlying the case being made is a highly Aristotelian way of construing the relationship of natures to persons. Philiponus acknowledges that groups of things can share a common nature but insists that that nature exists only in the form of individuals:

> Although the common and universal basis of man's nature is in itself one, nevertheless, since it is realized in several subjects, it is multiplied and exists not partially but wholly in each of these subjects.[37]

After defining *physis* as the common basis of all that share the same essence and presenting *hypostasis* as "the very individual real existence of each nature," noting that each individual has characteristics uniquely its own, Philoponus claims that *hypostasis* is irreducible to categories more basic yet. He explains why this should be so:

> This is because it is impossible further to divide any one of these [specified objects] into still other things which will continue to preserve the one same nature after the division. Thus the division of man into soul and body brings about the destruction of the complete animal.[38]

Nature then is seen as the larger category embracing the individual and not the other way around: natures encompass individual *hypostaseis*, but *hypostaseis* do not encompass natures.

The logic of this stance is extended even to the doctrine of the Trinity. There, Philoponus (nicknamed, we recall, the "Tritheite") finds the three *hypostaseis* as distinct and separable expressions of a common divine nature in a fashion analogous to the separateness of Peter and Paul as distinct

---

36. Joh.D., *Haer*. 13–19 (trans. Chase, 139).

37. The Greek text for this and the following excerpts from John Philoponus's *The Arbiter* can be found in Kotter, *Schriften*, 2:50–55 (trans. Chase, 140).

38. Chase, *Writings*, 140–41.

instances of a common human nature.[39] For it to be otherwise would entail, for him, some grave difficulties:

> For, what might the one nature of the Godhead be but the common basis of the divine nature as considered in itself and conceived as distinct from the peculiar property of each *hypostasis*? . . . For we certainly do not say that the nature of the Godhead which is understood as being common to the Holy Trinity was incarnate, for in such a case we would be declaring the incarnation of the Holy Ghost.[40]

The same reasoning is applied to the human nature united to the Logos:

> And neither do we hold the common essence of human nature to have been united to God the Word. For thus in the same way the Word of God could rightly be said to have been united both to the men living before His sojourn on earth and with those to come after.[41]

The reverse analogy found in John Damascene's Trinitarian thinking, whereby divine unity is more evident than diversity, has no place here. Rather, a particular way of construing the character and interrelationship of form and matter seems to dictate how both Trinitarian and christological matters are dealt with.

For Philoponus, nature and person are so closely linked that to have the former is, of necessity, to have the latter. If Christ does indeed have two natures, then he has two "persons" as well.[42] What he has is a unique divine-human nature that is expressed as his unique divine-human *hypostaseis*.[43]

That Philoponus might have been more extreme and not entirely representative of other monophysites, such as the more moderate Severus, is important to the history of thought but does not necessarily affect John Damascene's fundamental stance toward monophysitism, which was grounded in his own assessment of where the heart of the monophysite argument really lay. He faced not only centuries-old documents but living embodiments of positions that time doubtless altered in various ways.

Nestorianism and monophysitism, in a variety of manifestations, posed ongoing external challenges. But the classical Chalcedonianism that John embraced posed challenges of its own. By claiming that Christ was

39. Ibid., 142–43.
40. Ibid., 143.
41. Ibid., 143.
42. Ibid., 147.
43. Ibid., 144.

"of the same nature" (*homoousios*) as us, Chalcedon extended the range of explicit statements of the first two councils, as enshrined in the Niceno-Constantinopolitan Creed, and made the issue of a human nature in the Incarnation an urgent and pressing matter. Under the force of Apollinarianism, Gregory of Nazianzen laid down the classic soteriological rationale for full humanity: what has not been assumed cannot be healed.[44] Only a fully human Christ could heal the corruption and sin that ran through the whole of human nature, body and soul.

But the very faith of Nicea might seem to compromise that real and full humanity from the outset. Mary's virginal state, both in the conception and the birth of the incarnate Logos, might appear to undercut the insistence of the ecumenical statements that Christ had a full human nature.[45] How can a being begotten without a human father be truly human?

The uniqueness of Christ's conception and birth was seemingly not as troublesome for John as it might be for us. He devotes a whole chapter (chapter 12 in Book Three of *The Orthodox Faith*) to explicating the crucial role of Mary as "God-bearer" (*Theotokos*). The entire chapter centers on Mary's part in the Incarnation and not on any independent role she might be presumed to have in redemption.[46] What drives the argument is the logic of salvation: God (the Word) must truly be born; and he must be united to a genuine humanity.

John's position is set off, once again, against the backdrop of his ongoing polemic against Nestorianism and monophysitism. Nestorians balked at calling Mary the Mother of God or God-bearer and restricted her role to that of bearing Christ's humanity. John emphatically rejected this reduction:

> However, under no circumstance do we call the holy Virgin Mother of Christ [*Christokos*]. This is because that vessel of dishonor . . . Nestorius, invented this epithet as an insult to do away with the expression Mother of God and . . . to bring dishonor upon the Mother of God . . . And David is "Christ," too, and so is the high priest Aaron, because the royal and priestly offices are both conferred by annointing. Furthermore, any God-bearing

---

44. Gr.Naz., *Epistle 101* (*MPG* 37.181c), quoted in *OF* III.6.36–37 (trans. Chase, 280).

45. The Niceno-Constantinopolitan Creed, with its insistence on both the virgin birth and the assumption of humanity, is echoed in the Council of Ephesus (431), where Mary as *Theotokos* is a central issue, and at Chalcedon (451) where the humanity of Christ is even more strenuously proclaimed.

46. That John had other interests in Mary is attested to by his sermons on her birth and "falling asleep"; see Jean Damascene (S.), *Homilies sur la Nativité et la Dormition*, no. 89.

> [*Theophorus*] man may be called "Christ," yet he is not by nature God, which is why the accursed Nestorius was so insolent as to call Him who was born of the Virgin "God-bearing." But God forbid that we should ever speak or think of Him as God-bearing; rather, let it be as God incarnate. For the very Word of God was conceived of the Virgin and made flesh, but continued to be God after this assumption of the flesh. And, simultaneously with its coming into being, the flesh was straightway made divine by Him. Thus three things took place at the same time: the assuming of the flesh, its coming into being, and its being made divine by the Word. Hence, the holy Virgin is understood to be the Mother of God ....[47]

The lingering fear that John's tradition had of most forms of Antiochene Christology, including that extreme form allegedly adhered to by Nestorius, was that they ultimately reduced Christ to the level of an inspired prophet, though doubtless the greatest of all. The Chalcedonian mainstream insisted that the humanity joined to the Logos was none other than the Logos's own humanity: "For the holy Virgin did not give birth to a mere man but to true God, and not to God simply, but to God made flesh."[48] For this reason, the orthodox could confess that the Virgin was indeed the one who gave birth to the incarnate Word.

Monophysitism, in an extreme form, is likewise denied: "And He did not bring His body down from heaven and come through her as through a channel, but assumed from her a body consubstantial with us and subsisting in Himself."[49] Doubtless, John has the followers of the radical doctrine of Julian Haliacarnassus in view. As *Aphthartodocetae*, they denied Christ's body was truly human:

> ... [T]hey hold that the body of the Lord was incorruptible [*aphtharton*] from the first instance of its formation. They also confess that the Lord endured suffering—hunger, I mean, and thirst, and fatigue—but they say that He did not suffer these in the same way we do. For they say we suffer these by physical necessity, while the Christ suffered them voluntarily and was not subject to the laws of nature.[50]

It is in this context, an exposition of the essential role of the *Theotokos* that is at the same time a polemic against both Nestorians and monophysites, that

47. Joh.D. *OF* III.12.47–61 (trans. Chase, 294–95).
48. Joh.D. *OF* III.12.10–11 (trans. Chase, 292).
49. Joh.D. *OF* III.12.11–13 (trans. Chase, 292–93).
50. Joh.D. *Haer.* [*Aphthartodokatai*] 1–9 (trans. Chase, 148).

John Damascene clearly states the dominant sotereological rationale for the presence of full humanity in the Incarnation:

> Now, had the body been brought down from heaven and not been taken from our nature, was there any need for [the Word's] becoming man? God the Word was made for this reason: that the very nature which had sinned, fallen and become corrupt should conquer the tyrant who had deceived it.[51]

Not assumed means not healed. A full and real humanity had to be embraced in order for it to be "deified" by its union with the divine nature:

> Hence, the holy Virgin is understood to be Mother of God [*Theotokos*], and is so called not only because of the deification [*theosin*] of the humanity simultaneously with which the conception and the coming into being of the flesh were wonderously brought about—the conception of the Word, that is, and the existence of the flesh in the Word Himself. In this the Mother of God [*Theomateros*], in a manner surpassing the course of nature, made it possible for the Fashioner to be fashioned and the God and Creator of the universe to become man and deify [*theonti*] the human nature which he had assumed, while the union preserved the things united, just as they had been united, that is to say, not only the divinity of Christ but his humanity, also; that which surpassed us and that which is like us.[52]

A real birth, a truly human body, a full human nature: all of these were required by the conciliar tradition John Damascene embraced. Salvation of fallen humanity required that the Word enter into human reality, with all its physicality, even to the extent of developing within a womb and being born.

John does not back away from the implications of the oddity of claiming human birth for the Logos, who as one of the *hypostaseis* of the Trinity, had been and continues to be "begotten" of the Father. In chapter 7 of Book Three of *The Orthodox Faith*, he acknowledges the twofold character of Christ's begottenness:

> And we venerate His two begettings—one from the Father before the ages and surpassing cause and reason and time and nature, and one in latter times for our own sake, after our own manner, and surpassing us. For our own sake, because it was for the sake of our salvation; after our own manner, because He was made man from a woman with a period of gestation; and

---

51. Joh.D. *OF* III.12.13–18 (trans. Chase, 293).
52. Joh.D. *OF* III.12.60–68 (trans. Chase, 295).

> surpassing us, because, surpassing the law of conception, He was not from seed but from the Holy Ghost and the holy Virgin Mary.[53]

This statement encapsulates *in nuce* the underlying character and rationale of the Incarnation.

But a nagging question remains. Is a being undergoing human birth truly human without a human father as well? That John does not press the argument to this point suggests that the absence of a father does not trouble him as much as it might trouble us. Why this might be so can perhaps be illuminated by John's contention (discussed in our last chapter) that the different origins of the *hypostaseis* of the Trinity do not preclude their sharing a common nature any more than the different origins of Adam, Eve, and Seth prevented them from doing the same.[54] That point of view may well be the unstated argument undergirding the conviction that Christ's humanity was a real humanity despite the fact that it "surpassed the law of conception." Neither Adam nor Eve came into being in the (now) customary, and yet both are regarded as truly human and were capable of reproducing that true humanity.

What does it really mean, however, to have a full human nature directed, as it were, by the Logos? The concept of *enhypostasia* offers clarification at this point. As noted earlier, Leontius of Byzantium contended that a nature can be given personal form by being in a *hypostasis* that itself need not necessarily be an expression or extension of a single time or nature. Such an idea might at first glance seem obscure and far-fetched, but John Damascene's characterization in the *Philosophical Chapters* shows how it can be illustrated from ordinary human experience:

> In its proper sense . . . the *enhypostaton* is either that which does not subsist in itself but is considered in *hypostases*, just as the human species, or human nature, that is, is not considered in its own *hypostasis* but in Peter and Paul and other human *hypostases*. Or it is that which is *compound with another thing differing in substance to make up on particular whole and constitute one compound hypostasis*. Thus, a man is made up of soul and body, while neither the soul alone nor the body alone is called a *hypostasis*, but both are called *enhypostata* . . . Again, that nature is called *enhypostaton* which has been *assumed by another hypostasis and in this has its existence*. Thus, the body of the Lord, since it never subsisted of itself, not even for an instant, is not

---

53. Joh.D. *OF* III.7.30–36 (trans. Chase, 283).
54. Joh.D. *OF* I.8.119–22 (trans. Chase, 181; emphasis added).

a *hypostasis*, but an *enhypostaton*. And this is because it was assumed by the *hypostasis* of God the Word and this subsisted, and did and does have this for a *hypostasis*.[55]

An analogical relationship is suggested here between the conjunction of body and soul to form one *hypostasis*, on the one hand, and the uniting of human and divine natures in the one *hypostasis* of the Incarnation, on the other.

The connecting link, joining the Logos with human nature, is the human mind. For John Damascene, mind (*nous*) is not simply synonymous with soul (*psyche*). Even though it is part of the soul, it stands in a hierarchical relationship to both soul and body. In that position, it allows those "lower" parts to be connected with the Logos: "And so, the Word of God is united to the flesh by the intermediary of mind [*dia meous nou*] which stands midway between [*mesiteuonote*] the purity of God and the grossness [*pachutati*] of the flesh."[56] This passage, from chapter 6 of Book Three, goes on to proclaim an active function for Christ's human mind as well, all the while keeping it within the hierarchical relationship that maintains the primacy of the Logos:

> Now, the mind has authority over both body and should, but, whereas mind is the purest part of the body, God is the purest part of [Christ's human?] mind. And when the mind of Christ is permitted by the stronger, then it displays its own authority. However, it is under the control of the stronger and follows it, doing those things which the divine will desires.[57]

Within this hierarchy, the body is not disparaged, but it clearly has a subservient role to play in the hypostatic union.

How each of the elements of the body is united to each other and how a particular human body and soul are given personhood through the *hypostasis* of the Logos can be expressed and given some degree of intelligibility through the language of *enhypostasia*. All that is human in Jesus can be viewed as dwelling in the Word in fundamentally the same fashion that body is related to soul and soul is related to mind. Granting the terms of this particular psychological schema, one can glimpse the possibility that, just as mind (*nous*) can control soul (*psyche*), which in turn can control body (*soma*), without any of these elements being obliterated or suffering essential

---

55. Joh.D. *Dialectica* [*Peri enhypostatou*] 7–22 (trans. Chase, 68–69).
56. Joh.D. *OF* III.6.38–39 (trans. Chase, 280).
57. Joh.D. *OF* III.6.39–43 (trans. Chase, 280).

alteration in the process, so that the Logos may be viewed as embracing all of these human aspects without reducing any of them to insignificance.

It should be apparent that *enhypostasia* finds use in ways similar to *perichoresis*. Are the two words, in the various ways that they are employed, fundamentally equivalent? Each points to realities that are united without confusion. Clearly, there is some correspondence of meaning.

The match, however, is not perfect. One of the larger contentions of our study is that *perichoresis*, as John Damascene uses it, represents the culmination of a long struggle toward terminological clarification; it functions as a summing up of conceptual advances that had not all been made by the time Leontius of Byzantium gave *enhypostasis* the determinate shape it continues to have in discussions of Christology. Final clarity about wills and operations (see the following sections) took the Chalcedonian party another century and a half to reach. It was in the later era that *perichoresis* as a christological category came into its own, and it did so, not only in relation to the two natures in one *hypostasis*, but in terms of the two wills and two operations in the one Christ as well. For this reason, it took on a wider range of meanings than did *enhypostasia* and had a larger area of applicability.

One distinguishing characteristic of *perichoresis* is that it has a dynamic quality largely missing from *enhypostasia*. The latter term seems to imply a static relationship in which one thing rests in or is contained by another. *Perichoresis*, by contrast, implies a movement on the part of one or both natures.

G. L. Prestige, in one of the most influential studies of the character of *perichoresis*, points out earlier (pre-theological) usages of the term and argues that, in later patristic thought, *perichoresis* represents a movement, basically one-sided, toward (not in or through) the human object.[58]

Lars Thunberg, in his masterful study of Maximus the Confessor, disagrees. That his analysis of *perichoresis* focuses almost exclusively on Maximus does not make it inappropriate to our present discussion since John Damascene drew transparently on Maximus in his use of the term. What Thunberg finds inadequate in Prestige (and in H. Weser, who wrote in the nineteenth century) is a construal of *perichoresis* that allows the divine nature to act upon the human nature but gives no scope for human response.[59]

---

58. Prestige, *Patristic Thought*, 293.

59. Thunberg, *Microcosm and Mediator*, 24–25. Thunberg cites H. Weser's *S. Maximi, Confessoris Praecepta de Incarnatione Dei et Deificatione Hominis Exponutur et Examinatur*, diss., Halle-Berlin, 1869, 16. Thunberg's whole discussion of *perichoresis* is very illuminating and provided invaluable orientation to my study as a whole; see the section of chap. 1 titled "The Chalcedonian Heritage and Maximus' Theology of the Incarnation," *Microcosm*, 21–37.

Thunberg finds a more balanced position in the analysis of H. A. Wolfson, who recognizes that *perichoresis* involves penetration through (and not merely movement toward) and that it entails mutuality. Thunberg would go even further than Wolfson, who restricts mutual movement to the Incarnation, and find in the term (as used by Maximus and, by implication, John Damascene) the basis for a soteriological anthropology that invests a different importance to Christ's "human" activity.[60]

Even closer to Thunberg's liking is the position of Vladimir Lossky. Lossky argues for two stages in John's presentation of *perichoresis*:

> This *perichoresis*, or permeation, for St John Damascene, is *on the whole unilateral: comes from the divine side and not from the fleshly side. However, the Divinity,* having once *penetrated the flesh, gives to to it an ineffable faculty of penetrating the Divinity.*[61]

Lossky's argument is inferential: since *perichoresis* does not overwhelm the essential character of human nature, Christ's humanity continues to have a capacity for activity that it would not have if it were not joined to the Logos:

> When adoring my King and my God, I adore at the same time the porphyry of His Body—said the Damascene—not as a garment or as a fourth person, but as a body united to God, and abiding without change, as well as the divinity by which it has been anointed. For the corporal has not become God but, *just as the Word did not change and remained what he was through becoming flesh, so also the flesh became the Word without having lost what it had,* though it was identified with the Word in the hypostasis.[62]

The underlying anthropological vision here is one in which human nature, whether Christ's or ours, far from being diminished by its union with the divine nature, actually becomes fully itself.[63]

My reading of John Damascene favors the interpretation of Thunberg and Lossky; but regardless of whether one understands *perichoresis* in unilateral or bilateral terms, all conceptions entail the notion of dynamism.

---

60. Thunberg, *Microcosm,* 26. See also Wolfson, *Church Fathers,* 424–33.

61. Lossky, *Mystical Theology,* 145–46; emphasis added.

62. Lossky, *Mystical Theology,* 145–46; emphasis added, quoting Joh.D. *OF* IV.3 (cf. Chase, *Writings,* 336).

63. See Joh.D. *OF* III.17.16–19 (trans. Chase, 317), where the point is stressed that the Lord's flesh, rather than being disciplined (*ekptosin*), was actually enriched (*eploutase*) by the divine operations.

When that dynamism is attributed to both natures, however, it makes way for John's affirmation of Christ's two wills and operations.

How two natures could be united in one *hypostasis* without losing their separate identities and properties continues to be problematic after all that has been said. But the Incarnation, unlike the Trinity, provided John with certain analogical possibilities that were close at hand. As noted earlier, body and soul gave readily accessible illustration of two natures dwelling within a single *hypostasis*. Ancient science presented another model. In the *Philosophical Chapters*, John discusses various kinds of union (*Henosis . . . kata diaphorous tropous*). Among those he singles out for special comment are composition (*synthesin henosis*) and blending (*krasis*).[64]

The character of composition is set forth as follows:

> *Union by composition* is the mutual association [*perichoresis*] together of the parts without detriment to any of them, as in the case of the soul and the body. This is what some have called a blending together [*synkrasin*], that is to say, a knitting together [*symphuion*]. One must know, however, that while some of the Fathers did not accept the term blending in connection in connection with the Mystery of Christ, *union by composition was acceptable to them all.* This union which is by composition is the hypostatic union. That thing which subsists in two natures is one hypostatically. And again, that is one hypostatically which is perceived to be of two things but in one person. Still again, the union is hypostatic when the nature joins with another *hypostasis*.[65]

By affirming the hypostatic union, John aligns himself with received dogma. But the language he draws on to set forth his position has a close relationship to the philosophical/scientific legacy inherited from classical pagan thinkers.

The pioneering work of S. Sambursky is crucial in helping us see the relationship. In two important studies, he probes ancient physical theories and casts significant light especially on the advances Stoic physics makes on Aristotelian theory.[66] A brief examination of the way mixture (*mixis*) was construed in each of these two schools reveals an important body of ideas potentially available for John Damascene and other ancient Christian thinkers to draw on.

---

64. Joh.D. *Diatectica* [*Peri horou kai protaseos kai syllogismou*] (trans. Chase, 99–103).

65. Joh.D. *Dialectica* (trans. Chase, 104–13).

66. Sambursky, *Physical World* and *Physics of the Stoics*.

According to Sambursky's analysis, Aristotle found the very idea of mixture problematic. Mixture seemed to lack a homogeneous character because the attempt to mix two or more ingredients apparently resulted in mosaic-like composition, as results when, for instance, barley and wheat are combined. Such is the case with solids; the mixture of liquids creates an opposite situation. With liquids, the weaker of two substances is assimilated to the stronger and virtually disappears. A drop of wine in a large quantity of water provides a fitting example. In an age without sophisticated ways of chemical testing, that drop would seemingly have vanished without a trace. In Aristotelian terms, then, mixture represents either a mere "composition" (*synthesis*) or the absorption of one element by another.[67]

According to Sambursky, the later Stoics offered a clearer theory. Instead of two forms of mixture, they recognized three. (1) *Mingling* or *mechanical mixture* is equivalent to Aristotle's "composition" and marks out the character of what results when different kinds of grains are combined. (2) *Fusion*, at the other end, is the same as Aristotle's second type, in which either one element is lost to the other, if the ratio is overwhelmingly weighted on one side, or two elements combine into a third substance with the consequent loss of the distinctive characteristics of the elements going into the mixture. (3) *Mixture proper* or what the Stoics called "total mixture" (*krasis di'holon*) represents a new departure. Whether it involved liquids (krasis) or solids (mixis), for the Stoics it was the most important form of mixing. Sambursky describes it as follows:

> Here is a complete *interpenetration*[sic!] of all the components takes place, and any volume of the mixture, down to the smallest parts, is jointly occupied by all the components in the same proportion, *each component preserving its own properties under any circumstances, irrespective of the ratio of its share in the mixture.*[68]

Clearly, this third form of mixture suggests strong analogical connections with the hypostatic union of the two natures in the incarnate Word.

Perhaps the materialistic assumptions of Stoic thought, whereby even "spiritual" realities, such as spirit and soul, were believed to have a material basis, limited the attractiveness of parallels drawn from the physical world. Such may well have been the case with the monophysite Severus of Antioch. Roberta C. Chesnut notes his refusal to draw on analogies entailing the uniting of physical substances to illustrate the union of human and divine

---

67. Sambursky, *Stoics*, 11–12.
68. Ibid., 12–17; emphasis added.

in Christ because the incarnation represented the bringing together of two distinct levels of reality.[69]

How willing John Damascene might have been to draw on specifically Stoic ideas is hard to say. Of Stoicism, he offers this appraisal in *On Heresies*:

> The Stoics hold that the universe is a body and they think that this sensible world is God . . . They also define God as a mind which is at the [same] time the soul of the entire mass of heaven and earth.[70]

But the fact remains that the larger intellectual world of John's time provided a stock of ideas that could be drawn on, with critical caution, to give added intelligibility to the main Christian dogmas.

In the remainder of this section, we will examine *perichoresis* in two more specific contexts with the aim of reinforcing and extending what has already been said. The first passage is drawn from chapter 8 of Book Three of *The Orthodox Faith*:

> For the natures of Christ are two according to reason and the manner of the differences [*loigoi kai tropoi tas diaphoras*]. For they are held together by *hypostasis* and dwell within each other without confusion [*en allalais perichorasin echousai asyngkutos hanotai*], each individual nature saving [*diasoizousa*] its own intimate [*oikeian*], natural differences [*physikan diaphoran*].[71]

Read in the light of the last several pages, these words should take on a depth of meaning that might well not have been there for someone approaching the subject with scant knowledge of the basic concepts involved.

Among other things, we should recognize, on the basis of the larger context, that the *hypostasis* in the passage is the Logos. We should realize also that the Logos is the *hypostasis* of both natures, human and divine. Further, we should understand that the claim that each nature "saves" what is most intimately its own implies that the Logos, in John's view, does not diminish the full and real humanity of the created nature. Beyond this, we should be aware that each of these three assertions, along with others culled from other textual examples, is taken up into the christological application of *perichoresis* so that the term gains real density of meaning for those who carefully attend to how it is actually used.

Perichoresis, in the thought of John Damascene, functions as a magnet drawing various iron filings together into a coherent pattern. In the case

---

69. Chesnut, *Monophysite Christologies*, 18–19.
70. Joh.D. *Haer*. [*Stoikoi*] 1–4 (trans. Chase, 114).
71. Joh.D. *OF* III.8.19–24; my translation (cf. trans. Chase, 284–85).

of the "two natures/one person" conceptuality of Chalcedon, it is able to hold the language used to express it together in a more intelligible way by embracing, as part of its meaning, the clarifications provided by *enhypostasia* and the identification of the Logos as *hypostasis* of both natures and by adding a dynamic element to the penetrating power of each nature.

That dynamic element can be explicated in terms of the classical theological notion of the "exchange of properties" (*communicatio idiomatum*).[72] The following passage illustrates John's way of using the concept:

> Moreover, the Word makes human things his own, because what is proper to his holy flesh, belongs to him; and the things which are [naturally] his own [*idion*] he imparts [*metadidoi*] to his flesh. This is after the manner of exchange [*kata ton tas antidoseos tropon*] on account of the mutual indwelling of the parts [*dia tan eis allala ton meron merichorasin*] and the hypostatic union and because he who "with each form cooperating with [*koinonia*] the other" performed both human and divine acts was one and the same.[73]

The interior quotation is from Leo's *Tome*. It contains a word crucial to this passage: *koinonias*. Regardless of whether one chooses to translate that word as "communing with" or "fellowshipping with" or some other equivalent expression, *koinonias* necessarily carries some sense of activity or, at least, uncoerced responsiveness. Both parties, the human and the divine, are participant in the exchange, despite the suggestion of human passivity indicated by the opening sentence. Each nature preserves its own "natural" properties. What gives license to say of one nature what is antecedently true of the other nature is the hypostatically grounded unity of the one person of the incarnate Logos.

On the basis of the one *hypostasis* embracing both natures as truly its own, one can speak of the humanity of Jesus as if it were preexistent. By the same reasoning, one can say that the eternal Lord of Glory had been slain. Each saying applies to the whole Christ what in fact can only be strictly attributed to one of the natures. But, since each nature has only the Logos for its *hypostasis*, anything said of it or him automatically can be attributed to the other.

Grasping the communication of properties in the above fashion gives added fullness to the developed meaning of *perichoresis* and helps lay the

---

72. See the entry on "Communicatio Idiomatum/Communicatio Proprietatum" in Muller, *Latin and Greek Theological Terms*, 72–74.

73. Joh.D. *OF* III.3.75–80 (trans. Chase, 274).

The Presence of Two Wills in the Incarnate Word

The debate concerning whether Christ had one or two wills took its rise among Chalcedonians. One might speculate that a double concern underlay the advocacy of one will among some of those who affirmed two natures. One was the understandable wish to conciliate the monophysites, especially since the threat of Persia and, later, Islam brought about dramatic alterations to the Empire. The second concern was doubtless the fear that two wills implied a divided mind and, therefore, a move toward Nestorianism.[74] It took a powerful and creative imagination such as Maximus the Confessor possessed to see the wider and deeper implications raised by the issue and formulate a response that for many remains definitive.

John Damascene inherited Maximus's response and gave it classic expression in *The Orthodox Faith*. His teaching is expressed most fully in chapter 14 of Book Three, along with shorter treatments in chapters 17 and 18 of the same book.[75] In the first-named chapter, John says:

> Since, then, Christ has two natures, we say that He has two natural wills [*duo . . . physika thelmata*] and two natural operations [*duo . . . physikas energeias*]. On the other hand, since these two natures have one Person [*mia . . . hypostasis*], we say that He is one and the same who acts and wills naturally according to both natures . . . And we say that He wills and acts in each, not independently [*ou diairamenos*], but in concert [*hanomenos*]. "For in each form He wills and acts in communion [*koinonias*] with the other." For the will and the operation of things having the same substance [*ha ousia ha auta*] is the same, and the will and operation of things having different substance [*diaphoros ha ousia*] is different. Conversely, the substance of having the same will and operation is the same, whereas that of things having a different will and operation is different.[76]

---

74. The political threat from Persia and Islam finds description in Brown, *Late Antiquity*, esp. 160–203.

75. A much lengthier discussion can be found in John's *De Duabus in Christo Voluntatibus* (Greek text in Kotter, *Schriften*, 4:173–231). I have elected in this study to concentrate on John's ideas as presented in his most historically influential work and have, therefore, by-passed a close study of this treatise.

76. Joh.D. *OF* III.17.1–12 (trans. Chase, 296).

Perichoresis *and Christ* 77

In the interior quotation and the words that immediately follow, Boniface Kotter and Frederic H. Chase Jr. note the presence of Leo and Maximus respectively.[77] That those two names should be juxtaposed is illuminating. It ties the majority understanding of the Council of Chalcedon, with its ratification of Leo's *Tome*, to later developments, including the declarations of the Sixth Council.

For John and his tradition, the christological achievement of Chalcedon, controverted though it continued to be, set the terms for later achievements. The breakthroughs of the sixth and seventh centuries were framed within the conceptual boundaries laid out by Chalcedon. Two full and perfect natures united in one person without confusion or division continued to be enshrined and extended in the later conciliar proclamations.

A major thrust of our last chapter was to demonstrate that the Chalcedonian core—union without confusion—became foundational for John's Trinitarian thinking as well and was used by John to express the relationship of three *hypostaseis* to one *ousia* or *physis*. It is now time to examine a reciprocal move in which Christology draws on the insights of classical Trinitarianism to justify the presence of more than one will in the incarnate Logos.

In chapter 14 of Book Three, John claims a single nature is discernible in the Trinity: "Thus in the Father and Son and Holy Ghost, we discover the identity of nature from the identity of the operation and the will."[78] The Incarnation, by contrast, presents something else:

> In the divine Incarnation, on the other hand, we discover the difference of the nature from the difference of the wills and operations, and knowing the difference of the natures we confess the difference of the wills and operations. For, just as the number of natures piously understood and declared belong to the one and same Christ does not divide this Christ, but shows that the difference but shows that the difference of the natures is maintained even in the union, neither does the number of his wills *belonging substantially to His natures* introduce any division—God forbid—for in both of His natures He wills and acts for our salvation. On the contrary, their number shows the preservation and maintenance of the natures even in the union, and this alone. *We do not call the wills and operations personal but natural.* I am referring to that very *faculty of willing and acting by force of which things which will will and things which act*

---

77. Notes in both Kotter and Chase identify the sources as Leo, Epistle 28.4 (*MPG* 54.768B) and Maximus, *Disputation with Pyrrus* (*MPG* 91.313D–316A, 337B).

78. Joh.D. *OF* III.14.13–15 (trans. Chase, 296).

> act. For if we concede these to be personal, then we shall be forced to say that the three [hypostaseis] of the Holy Trinity differ in will and operation.[79]

The closing sentences of this passage provide us with a provisional definition of both will and operation. Together, they are identified as a "faculty" (actually "force" or "power"—*dynamin*) driving both volition and action. What each of these entails is best seen in the concrete circumstances of Christ's recorded life. John is in basic accord with Leo's *Tome*, which attributes certain aspects of Christ's activity to his divinity and other aspects to his humanity. How this division actually works out in John's exposition needs to be examined closely.

The gospels, especially the synoptics, give frequent recognition to the humanness of Christ's human nature: he thirsts, hungers, tires, angers, and so on. Most of these traits could be accomodated within a Logos-sarx framework in which the incarnate Word assumes the "burden" of a (perhaps mindless) human body. The inadequacy of such a framework becomes apparent in those contexts that reveal that Christ not only "suffers" certain things (ie he experiences them in a basically passive way) but also "wills" things at times in such a way that both the reality and the limitations of his humanness are revealed. Mark's gospel (7:24) provides an example:

> And . . . as the holy Gospel relates, the Lord went "into the coast of Tyre and Sidon: and entering : and entering into a house, *He would that no man should know it. And He could not be hid.*" So if His divine will was all-powerful [*pantodynamon*] and yet He was unable [*dedynatai*] to conceal Himself when He willed to, then it was willing as a man. [*katho anthropos thelasas*] that He was unable to, and as a man also He was volitive [*thelatikos*].[80]

But perhaps a more theologically urgent example is the struggle with the prospect of death that we glimpse as Christ prays in the Garden of Gethsemane. In chapter 18 of Book Three, John offers a most interesting assessment of that dramatic struggle. He begins with an affirmation of the reality of Christ's human soul, which is nevertheless ruled by the Logos, and the existence of a human will, which likewise bowed to the divine will:

> So, the Lord was not made flesh without soul or mind, but He made himself man. In fact, He says: "Why do you seek to kill me, a man who have spoken to you?" Therefore, He assumed a body animated by a rational and intellectual *soul having dominion*

---

79. Joh.D. *OF* III.14.15–29 (trans. Chase, 296–97; emphasis added).
80. Joh.D. *OF*, III.14.99–103 (trans. Chase, 100; emphasis added).

> over the flesh, but itself being under the dominion of the divinity of the Word. . . . Consequently, while He had naturally the *power of willing both as God and man, the human will followed after and was subordinated to His will*, not being motivated by its own opinion, but willing what His divine will willed.[81]

If the divine will is dominant, what then takes place in Gethsemane? A careless reading of John Damascene might lead one to conclude that the scene in the Garden would have to represent, for him, the divine will at odds with itself. John reveals something else at work:

> Thus it was with the permission of the divine will that He suffered what was naturally proper to Him. And *when He begged to be spared death, He did so naturally, with His divine will willing and permitting, and He was in agony and afraid.* Then, when His human will willed that *His divine will chose death, the passion was freely accepted by it, because it was not as God alone that He freely delivered Himself over to death, but as man also.*[82]

Several factors are at work here. Ordinarily, the divine will prevails over the human will which, nevertheless, willingly accepts its subordinate role. On occasion, however, the human will is allowed to reveal itself. When it does, it displays its "natural" tendencies, such as fear, hunger, and so on. These responses still permit the human will to acquiesce to the intent of the divine will.

If the divine will always prevails, what function does a human will really perform? John places the issue in the context of "not assumed/not healed." The will is among those things needing healing in fallen human nature. The human will that briefly comes to the fore in Gethsemane is given the power to face and accept death:

> Whence, He also gave us courage in the face of death. Thus, indeed, He says before His saving passion: "Father, if it is possible, let this chalice pass from me." It is *manifestly as a man* that He was to drink the chalice, for it was *not as God*. Consequently, it is as a man that He wishes the chalice to pass, and these are words arising from a natural fear. "But yet not my will, but thine be done," that is to say: "In so far as I am of another substance than thine, but thine, which is mine, and thine in so far as I am consubstantial with thee." Again, these are words of courage. For, since by His good pleasure the Lord had become truly man,

---

81. Joh.D. *OF* III.18.28–32 (trans. Chase, 319; emphasis added),
82. Joh.D. *OF* III.18.36–40 (trans. Chase, 319–20; emphasis added).

> His soul at first experienced the weakness of nature and through sense perception felt a natural pain at the thought of its separation from the body; then it was strengthened by the divine will and faced death courageously. For since He was entirely God with His humanity and entirely man with His divinity, He as man in Himself and through Himself subjected His humanity to God the Father and became obedient to the Father, thus setting for us a most noble example and pattern.[83]

The human will is here given a real and positive function whereby it freely assents to that which it "naturally" abhors and does so, not only to set a "most noble example and pattern," but also to embrace human fear in the face of impending death (and torture) and thereby sanctify that fear with grace. The joining of human and divine wills allows divinity to transform the humanity, which in turn becomes savingly available to the rest of humanity.

The soteriological rationale for the hypostatic union of two natures, each with its own will, finds expression in many different contexts. Chapter 6 of Book Three lays out the principle very clearly and masterfully, especially in this terse statement echoing Gregory of Nazianzen: "He in His entirety assumed me in my entirety and was wholly united to the whole. For that which has not been assumed cannot be healed."[84] The necessity of embracing our experience at its very depth in order to bring it into the realm of redemption underscores the reality of Christ's human suffering. That that suffering was voluntarily endured and could, so to speak, be set aside does not diminish its reality. For John, the suffering really happened and it was part of the real experience of the humanity of the Word.

Superficially, John Damascene's affirmation of Christ's suffering as voluntary and, apparently, intermittent might seem to link John with the *Aphthartodocetae*, whom John places on his list of heresies. As noted earlier, these were extreme monophysites associated with the thought of Julian of Haliacarnassus. What set them apart from the more moderate Severus of Antioch is that "...they hold that the body of the Lord was incorruptible from the first instant of its formation ... we suffer [certain things like hunger and fatigue] by physical necessity, while Christ suffered them voluntarily and was not subject to the laws of nature."[85]

Two things set John's position apart from this heresy. While both sides agree that Christ's sufferings were voluntary, John did not believe Christ's body had been incorruptible, nor did he separate that body from the

---

83. Joh.D. *OF* III.18.40–56 (trans. Chase, 320; emphasis added).
84. Joh.D. *OF* III.6.35–37 (trans. Chase, 280).
85. Joh.D., *Dialectica* [*Aphthartodokatai*] 1–9 (trans. Chase, 148).

limitations of the laws of nature. Positively, John understood the character of Christ's voluntary sufferings in two ways: the Logos freely entered the limitations of human experience in the Incarnation; and Christ was free to suspend those limitations at certain moments in his incarnate life.

But a certain question persists: How does a human mind will if it is not, at the same time, a person? This was the abiding query of the Antiochene tradition. The answer of John and the broad Alexandrian tradition that he inherited is that it is indeed a person—the person of the Logos. Unless this is grasped, the so-called Neo-Chalcedonian viewpoint (ie the view that stresses Cyril's emphasis on the unity of the person of Christ more emphatically than it does the Antiochene accent on the two natures) appears to join a personal divinity with an impersonal humanity.

In a certain sense, John might have accepted the characterization of "personal divinity/impersonal humanity." In his *Philosophical Chapters*, he defines the term *anhypostaton* as that which either has no existence or, more important for our purpose, has no existence of its own.[86] In the second sense, *anhypostaton* stands in close relationship to *enhypostasia*. Each can indicate that which has its existence in another.

The human will for John, then, exists in the *hypostasis* of the Logos. To affirm such, however, is not to claim that the Logos directs that will—from the outside, so to speak—in a way that renders it inoperative. That will is the Logos's own (human) will; in this sense, there is no inside/outside. But, more importantly for our present concern, the human will of the Logos, when given scope, responds in a "naturally" human way.

A capacity for willing is intrinsic to the human nature. John makes a clear distinction between willing as a capacity and the actual exercise of the will:

> Now, one must know that *willing* is not the same as *how one wills*. This is because will . . . is *of the nature*, since it belongs to all men. *How one wills*, however, does *not belong to nature but to our judgment* . . . Consequently, simple willing is called *will*, or the volitive faculty, which is a natural will and rational appetite. But how one wills . . . is the object willed and will be based on judgment. And that is *volitive* which has it *in its nature to will*. For example, the divine nature is volitive, and so is the human. And, finally, he is willing who uses the volition and that is *the person*; Peter, for example.[87]

---

86. Joh.D., *Dialectica* [*Anhypostatou*] 1–3 (trans. Chase, 69).
87. Joh.D. *OF* III.14.30–42 (trans. Chase, 297; emphasis added).

The capacity to will is linked with the nature, while the judgment that comes into play in actual instances of willing is tied to the person.

It is here that the Trinitarian parallel breaks down into mere analogy since the correspondence between *physeis* and *hypostaseis* in the Trinity and the Incarnation is tenuous at best. The tradition of Maximus and the Sixth Council that John draws on identified the (common) nature as the locus of the will in the Trinity but did not go on to argue that the three *hypostaseis* each possessed individual judgment. For this reason, one can only use "person" as a translation of *hypostasis* (in relation to the Trinity) in a highly qualified way, which is why I have generally left *hypostasis/hypostaseis* untranslated.

John, of course, acknowledged the unparalleled character of the Trinity. Much of our second chapter was taken up with presenting John's view of the discontinuous relationship of the divine essence in its three-fold being to the world. What the seventh-century advocates of two wills did was seize on one aspect of Trinitarian being where analogical speech seemed possible and use that aspect as a *modus vivendi* for arguing toward the duality of wills in Christ. What Trinitarian reflection did was suggest that certain possibilities of relationship were seen to have connections with christological problems.

Underlying the increasingly sophisticated technical argument for the plurality of wills was the need, generated by the gospel narratives, to account for such things as Christ's ambivalence toward his impending execution. The narratives move in seemingly contradictory directions that could not be ignored. The authoritative status of the gospels required that some equally authoritative response be given that would allow all the parts to be held together in a satisfactory way.

Once again, *perichoresis* provided a way of bringing contraries together in union without violating their final differences. If there is a mutual indwelling of human and divine natures in Christ, then there must also be a mutual indwelling of wills as well, since dogmatic opinion posited that the wills resided in the natures.

In the relationship of mutual indwelling, both the human nature and the human will were deified without being transformed into something else:

> One should know that it is not by a transformation of nature [*metabolan physeos*] or by change or alteration or mingling that the Lord's flesh is said to have been deified [*tetheosthai*] and made identical with God [*homotheos*] . . . This was by no transformation of nature but by the union through dispensation [i.e. the Incarnation], the hypostatic union . . . and by them mutual

> indwelling of the natures [*en allalais ton physeon perichoresin*] . . . For, just as we confess that the Incarnation was brought about without transformation or change, so also do we hold that the deification [*theosin*] of the flesh was brought about . . . [W]hen the flesh was made divine, it certainly did not change its own nature or its natural properties. . . . Likewise, we say that the *deification of the will* was not by a transformation of its natural motion, but by its being united with His divine and almighty will and being the will of God made man.[88]

The human will maintains its basic character all the while being part of the one Christ. Mutual indwelling allows both wills, the human and the divine, to unite without confusion.

Once again, *perichoresis* expands, as it were, to take in the meaning of a newly articulated insight, which in turn becomes part of the meaning of *perichoresis* in many of the contexts where it is later put to use. Identity and difference, the identity of the incarnate person and the differences of the wills, viewed in the light of mutual indwelling, gave new depth to Chalcedon and brought more clarity to the diversity of the two natures in the incarnate Logos. Our final section will examine how John attempts to make the same use of the concept of two operations.

The Reality of Two Operations in the Incarnate Word

John of Damascus's principal discussion of energies or operations is found in chapters 15 and 19 of Book Three of *The Orthodox Faith*. In the former chapter, John lays down some basic distinctions:

> Operation [*energeia*] . . . is the efficacious and substantial motion [*ha drastika kai ousiodas kinasis*] of the nature. And that which is operative [*energatikon*] is the nature from which the operation proceeds. That which is operated [*energama*] is the effect of the operation. And the operator [*energon*] is the one who performs the operation; the person [*hypostasis*], that is. However, the term operation is also used for the effect, and the term for the effect for the operation, as "creation" is used for "creatures." For in this way we say "all creation," meaning "all creatures."[89]

Working with these distinctions, John proceeds to clarify the character of operation further in order to avoid possible misunderstandings:

88. Joh.D. *OF* III.17.1–28 (trans. Chase, 316–17; emphasis added).
89. Joh.D. *OF* III.15.6–10 (trans. Chase, 304).

> One must know that the operation is a motion and that it is operation is a motion and that it is operated upon rather than operating ... It is further necessary to know that life itself is an operation, and the primary operation of the animal. So also is the whole vital process ... Operation, moreover, is the perfection of a potentiality. So, if we find these things [i.e., the characteristic activities of living beings] in Christ, then we shall declare that He also has a human operation.[90]

Through these various discriminations, a picture emerges of operation as a force that is, nevertheless, not self-directed. How convincing that description is in light of various involuntary functions of the body depends, perhaps, on whether the operator is construed as the embodied creature or as the presiding Creator. In either case, it should be noted that each operation reflects the type of nature from which it is derived: humans have one kind of operation, non-human creatures have another, and divinity has its own.

Another series of clarification follows that shows operation spread out over a continuum reaching from pure thought at one end all the way to physical action at the other:

> The first thought [*noama*] in us is called operation. It is a simple unrelated operation by which the mind of itself secretly puts forth those thoughts of its own without which it could not rightly be called mind [*nous*]. And again, that is also called an operation which is the expression and explanation of what has been thought by means of speech utterance. This, however, is no longer unrelated and simple. On the contrary, since it is combined of thought and speech, it is found to be in a relation. And the very relation which the doer has to the thing is also an operation. And the thing itself which is effected is called an operation. Now, the first of these belongs to the soul alone, the next to the soul as using the body, the next to the body as endowed with an intellectual soul, and the last of them is the effect.[91]

This nicely laid out progression gives us the categories for identifying the possible types of specifically human operation. Only humanity, with its mixture of thought and embodiment, has the potential of moving from idea to physical action in the manner outlined above.

Divinity has its own operation which is most strongly evident in displays of the miraculous. Christ manifested both kinds of operation. John Damascene offers a striking example found in Matthew 8:2–3:

90. Joh.D. *OF* III.15.13–16 (trans. Chase, 304).
91. Joh.D. *OF* III.15.27–31 (trans. Chase, 305).

> And behold a leper came to [Jesus] and knelt before him saying, "Lord, if you will, you can make me clean." And he stretched out his hand and touched him, saying, "I will; be clean."[92]

John finds four elements in Christ's response: the touching, the willing, the speaking, and the healing itself. For John, only the last of these belongs to the divine nature; the other three are manifestations of human will and operation.[93]

John goes on to explain the underlying unity of both human and divine operations in Christ's ministry:

> Now, by both, that is, by the operation of the soul and that of the body, He showed His divine operation to be one and the same, akin and equal. And just as we know that the natures are united and mutually immanent [*perichoresin*] and still do not deny their difference, but even number them, while we know them to be indivisible; so also do we know the connection of the wills and operations, while we recognize their difference and number them without introducing any division. For as the flesh was made divine, yet suffered no change it its own nature, in the same way the will and operations were made divine, yet did not exceed their proper limits.[94]

As with the duality of the wills, John infers the duality of the operations from the two-ness of the natures:

> Accordingly, because of the duality of His nature, it is necessary to affirm two operations in Christ. For things having diverse natures have different operations, and things having different operations have different natures.[95]

As one of our passages indicates, it is mutual immanence that holds the operations together, allowing us to think of them as one, just as we can link the two natures and the two wills.

Another concept that advanced clarity is that of "theandric operation" (*theandrika energeia*).[96] John inherited this notion from a tradition extending back through Maximus to Pseudo-Dionysius. He explains it in chapter 19 in Book Three:

---

92. Joh.D. *OF* III.15.40–44 (trans. Chase, 305).
93. Joh.D. *OF* III.15.43–52 (trans. Chase, 305).
94. Joh.D. *OF* III.15.43–52 (trans. Chase, 305–6).
95. Joh.D. *OF* III.15.55–57 (trans. Chase, 306).
96. Joh.D. *OF* III.19 (trans. Chase, 321–23).

> When the blessed Dionysius said that Christ had used a certain new theandric operation with us, he was not doing away with the natural operations and saying there was proceeding from the human and the divine natures. For, if such were the case, we might also say that there was one new nature made from the human and the divine, because, according to the Fathers, things which have one operation also have one substance. On the contrary, he wanted to show that *the new and ineffable manner of the manifestation of the natural operations in Christ* was consonant with *the mutual indwelling of Christ's natures in each other*, and that His living as a man was both unusual and incredible and unknown to the nature of things. He also wanted to show the *manner of the exchange* arising from the ineffable union. Thus, we do not say that the operations are separated and that the natures act separately, but we say that they act conjointly, with each nature doing in communion with the other that which is proper to itself.[97]

In light of Dionysius' presumed monophysitism, either John is reading alien meanings into Dionysius or the moderate monophysite approach of the Areopagite (and Severus) is much closer to the intent of the later advocates of Chalcedon than either side was prepared to recognize. In either case, John's own aim is clear: he wishes to affirm the ultimate congruence of Christ's human and divine actions and does so with the aid of the language not only of mutual indwelling but of theandric operation, exchange of properties, and communion as well. Each of these gives expression to the Chalcedonian concern for union without confusion.

Mutually indwelling operations represent a way of acting that is neither strictly human nor divine but a combination of both. Detractors of Chalcedon had seen in the Leo's *Tome* a tendency to group Christ's actions, in an overly neat way, under the heading of either human or divine. John Damascene, following Dionysius, will have none of that:

> [Christ] did not perform the human actions in a human way, because He was not a mere man, nor did He perform the divine actions in a divine way only, because He was not just God, but God and man together. And just as we understand both the union of natures and their natural difference, so also do we understand that of the natural wills and operations.[98]

---

97. Joh.D. *OF* III.19.1–14 (trans. Chase, 321–22; emphasis added).
98. Joh.D. *OF* III.19.14–19 (trans. Chase, 322).

Such language might suggest some form of monophysitism. But John guards against that by carefully defining theandric operation is such a way that Christ's two natures both come into play, usually in a simultaneous fashion, but in a manner that permits one to distinguish between the two. What allows the two operations to act in concert is their mutual indwelling.

Perichoresis now encompasses, not only the advances of the fifth and sixth centuries, but the new insights gained in the seventh as well. The duality of wills and operations takes its place in post-Chalcedonian interpretation along with *enhypostasia* and the Logos as the *hypostasis* of the two natures. All of these moves toward clarification are themselves clarified by the concept of mutual indwelling. Without it, the balance between identity and difference tends to break down in either a Nestorian or monophysite direction.

Having laid out John of Damascus's articulation of *perichoresis* in terms of the Trinity and the Incarnation, we now turn to his understanding of salvation to see what role mutual indwelling might play there.

4
Perichoresis and Salvation

PERICHORESIS PLAYS A CENTRAL ROLE IN THE ARTICULATION OF BOTH THE Trinitarian theology and the Christology of John of Damascus. It serves to focus the Chalcedonian character (unity without confusion) of both doctrines. The time has now come to ask how such language might apply to the issue of salvation. John is far less helpful here because his soteriological teachings are not presented with the same directness. *The Orthodox Faith*, with its primary concentration on God and Christ, touches on many other matters as well, but its words on the saving significance of Christ have to be gleaned in contexts that have other topics for their main concern.

The strategy of what follows, then, will have to be that of turning to creation, baptism, the eucharist, and other issues where some kind of union between God (or Christ) and humanity is featured. Along with *perichoresis*, a new category, participation (in one or another of its various forms), will figure in the discussion. Participation, broadly speaking, is that notion, taken from Platonic thought, that bespeaks of one reality reflecting and "dwelling in" an archetypal form of that same reality, as when an individual chair is said to participate in the ideal form of "chairness."[1]

After a preliminary discussion of the relationship of *perichoresis* to various notions of participation, we will examine John's teaching in the following sequence:

> Humanity's orginal union with God
> The loss of union with God through the Fall
> Union regained through Christ's redemption
> Final union with God in the life to come

---

1. See the brief but illuminating discussion of participation in Armstrong, *Ancient Philosophy*, 39–40; and Allen, *Philosophy for Understanding*, 20–21, 86, 143.

As we do so, we will be tracing out John's characteristically Eastern Christian understanding of salvation as *theosis* or "deification," a rich body of ideas that entails far more than the forgiveness of sins and the meritorious righteousness, whether infused or imputed, essential to most Western approaches. As we do so, we will inquire as to what kind of applicability *perichoresis* might have in relation to another instance of diverse realities being united.

Perichoresis or Participation?

Given the fact that John Damascene nowhere in *The Orthodox Faith* speaks of personal salvation in terms of mutual indwelling, the legitimacy of this chapter might be questioned at the outset. The previous chapters have assiduously attempted to limit the primary meanings of *perichoresis* to those contexts where the term clearly figures. But those meanings have had implications for other contexts as well, and *perichoresis* has been urged as a major way of gathering up the structural elements of John's theological and christological thought and giving them added coherence and focus, without which they might tend to fragment into isolated notions without real systematic force. That *perichoresis* has ramifications for soteriology as well will be argued by comparing it with the distinctly different, and yet related, concept of participation. In doing so, we will draw heavily on the seminal work of David L. Balas.[2]

David Balas, in a study that focuses primarily on Gregory of Nyssa, examines participation in its various Greek forms, both in ancient philosophical and patristic Greek contexts. His treatment of the classical heritage is cursory, but it is sufficient to root participation in Plato's teaching of the relationship of the ideal forms to the multiplicity of objects found in the visible world.[3] *Methexis* is the primary word used to express that relationship, but it stands next to a small number of other words that, in their various contexts, set forth the same or similar meanings.[4]

Balas notes adaptations of "participation" in Aristotle and the Stoics but is especially keen to focus on the uses found in the later Platonists. The hierarchical ordering of the world that emerged in Middle and Neo-Platonism extended the range of participation beyond that of connection

---

2. See Balas, *METOUSIA THEOU*. Note should be made here of an excellent monograph by Winslow, *Dynamics*, especially the eighth chapter ("Theosis"), 171–99.

3. Balas, *METOUSIA THEOU*, 1–6.

4. Ibid., 2. Among these are *metocha, metechein, metalambanein, metelapsis,* and near-synonyms such as *koinonia* and *koinonein*.

between the world of ideas and sensible being; in the elaborate ladder of reality constructed by later thinkers, participation brought together all the levels of the hierarchy: each lower reality was envisioned by Plotinus and others as "dwelling" within the reality immediately above it.[5] Participation, in its later philosophical developments, is therefore a way of articulating an ontological continuum that ties together the highest and lowest reaches of being through a plethora of intermediate forms.

How well do such notions fit with the Christian scriptures? Balas briefly notes the most obvious points of possible contact. In the New Testament, a focused philosophical interest is, of course, absent. But the language of participation is present in crucial places and is used to express a number of relationships.[6] Among these are Christ's participation in our mortality, our participation in him, our participation in his body and blood in the eucharist, our fellowship with the Holy Spirit, and our participation in the divine nature.[7] The last named is especially striking because it might appear to foreshadow patristic expressions of the indwelling of the divine *hypostaseis* in the divine nature or *ousia*. But, as Balas observes, these scriptural usages, all of them, have specifically soteriological references and give definition to the character of the salvation found in Christ.[8]

Patristic appropriation of participation language reflects both the philosophical and biblical legacies. A second-century example, Justin Martyr, accented the philosophical strand by his linking of God and humanity through the Logos that indwells all humans, thereby implying an immanental connection between Creator and creation.[9] On the one hand, his younger contemporary, Irenaeus, can make extensive use of participation while seemingly by-passing the philosophical usages altogether. He speaks rather of participation in life or in the Spirit in ways clearly indebted to the conceptuality of the Bible.[10]

The Platonic influence is much more pronounced in Origen, who, in the following century, used the ideas of his philosophical teachers to construe participation in hierarchical terms, whereby the different levels of reality could be joined; even the Son and the Spirit received their divinity in a derived and subordinate fashion through their participation in the "higher" reality of the Father. The Son and the Spirit, in turn, convey salvation to

5. Ibid., 3–5.
6. Ibid., 6–7.
7. Ibid., 6.
8. Ibid., 7.
9. Ibid., 8.
10. Ibid., 9.

creatures when the latter participate in them.[11] It is here, with the participation of humanity with God, that the way is marked out for the use of participation language in later patristic thought.

This narrowing of the range of applicability appears in Gregory of Nyssa. Despite the Origenistic aspects of Gregory's thought, his view of the restoration of creation for instance, his thinking also reflected that sharp cleavage between God and creation that Athanasius, his earlier contemporary, had articulated so forcefully in the Arian controversy.[12] It is that cleavage that moves Gregory to restrict participation to relationships existing between humanity and God and to exclude those relationships within God or between God and the humanity of the Word.

Why Gregory should place the Incarnation beyond the range of participation is manifested in connection with a series of contrasting terms that Balas uses to bring out important differences:

> "By participation" versus "by itself"
> Composition versus simplicity
> "More or less" versus infinity
> Mutability versus immutability
> Temporality versus eternity[13]

These form the sub-headings for the fifth chapter of Balas's study. The first term in each pair marks out some aspect to the character of participation. Since each bears a close connection with the ways in which John Damascene treats participation, we will briefly summarize them in turn.

(1) Under the first head, "by participation" versus "by itself," Balas says, ". . . to participate means to have acquired, to have received from without, though not necessarily in a passive and unconscious manner."[14] Such a description obviously excludes the interrelationships of the *hypostaseis* of the Trinity but seems a possible characterization of the humanity of the Word, which was the recipient of that which was not itself. Gregory apparently did not use the idea in that way, as the remaining terms make clear.

(2) Composition is poised over against simplicity, in part, in order to make clear that the participant is distinct from that which is participated. Unlike God, who does not participate in goodness or any

---

11. Ibid., 9–11.
12. Ibid., 11–12.
13. See the headings in ibid., chap. 5, pp. 121–40.
14. Ibid., 124.

other perfection because each perfection is simply God's nature, humans are separable from the qualities they might come to share.[15] Only within a subordinationist framework, such as that advocated by Eunomius, could such a conception of participation be applied to the Trinity,[16] but there may still appear to be a possible application to the Incarnation. Christ's human nature shared in qualities clearly external to its "natural" character. The next pair adds an important qualification.

(3) "More or less" is contrasted with infinity, a distinction that illuminates the difference between the uncreated nature of God and the created, variable nature of humans. Human nature can be called good only insofar as it participates in God's goodness; it has no intrinsic goodness that it can somehow claim as a possession.[17] Because it is variable, ordinary human nature can move in and out of that relationship. Christ's human nature, by contrast, is not variable. Later developments, known to John Damascene but presumably unknown to Gregory of Nyssa, explained Christ's steadfast humanity in terms of its being under the direction of the Logos, thereby sharing in the latter's constancy.

(4) Mutability versus immutability essentially underscores the same contrast: to be part of the created world is necessarily to be part of the flux and inconstancy that characterize all reality outside of God.[18] By taking on a corruptible body (i.e., one subject to death and dissolution), Christ, in some sense, also shared in mutability; but his human nature, with the Logos as its subject, received steadfastness and was, therefore, in no danger of falling away.

(5) The final pairing, temporality in contrast to eternity, simply suggests the created/uncreated distinction from yet one more angle. All five contrasts, in one way or another, focus on the "insurmountable interval" implied in that distinction.[19] Once again, humans can only lay claim to the second term in a a derivative and non-binding way. As for Christ, both sides of the divide are brought together but in

15. Ibid., 124.
16. Ibid., 125.
17. Ibid., 135.
18. Ibid., 136–37.
19. Ibid., 137.

such a way that the limitations of the first term are transcended, though not in a manner that destroys natural properties.

How then does participation, at least as we find it in Gregory of Nyssa, fit in with *perichoresis*, understood as "mutual indwelling"? There is clearly an overlap in meaning, but there are differences as well. Leaving aside the interrelationships of the Trinity, for which earthly parallels are hard, if not impossible, to come by, some connection can be found between the bringing together of Christ's two natures, on the one hand, and the conjunction of humanity and God either in creation or in salvation, on the other. Each unites divinity and humanity; each bridges in some way the seemingly unbridgeable gap between God and the world. But participation, as Gregory of Nyssa (and others to follow) uses it, apparently is limited to that relationship that exists when human beings are truly related to God through Christ.[20]

Balas's case rests on the copious citations he has culled from Gregory's extant writings; the same case will be attempted for John Damascene but will have to be far more inferential because participation language, in *The Orthodox Faith*, is hardly pervasive or of central concern to the passages where it is found. What is beyond question is that the language of mutual indwelling is never used by John apart from clear reference either to the union of the *hypostaseis* of the Trinity or that of the two natures of Christ.

Perichoresis, then, has as its basic references either God or the incarnate Word. The previous two chapters have either exhibited or alluded to every instance in *The Orthodox Faith* that makes use of *perichoresis* or any of its derivative forms. Never is the word used to identify the bond that exists between God and the created world or the saving relationship that unites baptized believers to God (or Christ or eternal life). Before turning to the language that is used by John to express such relations, a venture should be made to explain why participation and *perichoresis* occupy somewhat different places on the terminological map.

The basic clue for this difference of locale in these two terms might lie in the origin of the philosophical use of participation. Without suggesting that earlier meanings of words somehow rest latent or dormant in later usages, one can note the persistent influence of Plato, especially in his theory of ideas. Even though later thinkers put that theory to a variety of uses probably not contemplated by Plato, it became a stock way of expressing the relationship of particular realities to the larger reality of which they apparently formed a part. Even the Aristotelian rejection of ideal forms as somehow

20. Ibid., 139–140.

existing apart from actual substances nevertheless saw individual things as fitting into species, each of which could be located within a genus.[21]

Running through both earlier and later understandings of participation, then, is the common theme of a part being related to a whole. Never might the part claim to embrace the totality of the group that gives it its identity. The participant is always partial and lacks the fulness of some larger totality, be it an eternal form, a higher element in the hierarchy of being, a species or genus, or (in biblical usage) the uncreated personhood found in divinity.

The language of "lesser part in larger whole" clearly diverges, then, from what might be said of John Damascene's understanding of the relationship of the Trinity to the Godhead. the classical Christian view of God set forth in our second chapter proclaims the fullness of divine being in each of the three *hypostaseis*: apart from the manner of their respective origins, each is fully, completely, and perfectly God and subsists in a common nature that precludes one *hypostasis* possessing what another lacks. The language to describe that "diversity in unity" is the vocabulary of mutual indwelling.

The same might be said, though less unambiguously, of the Incarnation. Though Christ's human nature was created and, therefore, "inferior" to his divine nature, it was, from the very moment of conception, *his* human nature and not something outside of himself. The Logos united both natures in the one person of Christ. Neither nature is somehow alien to the union or in danger of falling away. True, each nature preserves its own distinctive identity and neither, in some manner, becomes the other; but they are so closely linked that each can claim the qualities of the other as part of its common self.

Participation, by contrast, bespeaks of a relativity, a separateness of the participant from that in which it participates, that points to various types of union far less stable and complete. Several types come into view in *The Fount of Knowledge* and will be presented and analyzed, in the remaining sections, in terms of the drama of creation, fall, and redemption.

Humanity's Original Union with God

John Damascene's incidental references to participation of one sort or another fit well into the sequence from creation to final redemption. Both the beginning and the end of humanity's relationship with God entail the imparting of God's uncreated life to created beings. Our second chapter emphasized the enormous gap between Creator and created but postponed

21. See Armstrong, *Ancient Philosophy*, 77–86.

until now discussion of the created link between God and the world. Chapter 2 of Book Two of *The Orthodox Faith* gives a glimpse of that relationship:

> Now, because the good and more than good God [*ho agathos kai hyperagathos theos*] was not content [*ouk arkestha*] to contemplate Himself [*tai heautou theoriai*], but in exceeding goodness saw fit that there should be some things to benefit and *participate in His goodness* [*methexonta tas autou agathotatas*], He brings all things from nothing into being and creates them, both visible and invisible, and humanity, which is made of both.[22]

The essential point to note here is creation's *participation* (*metaxonta*) in God's goodness. But note should also be made that John posits as the basis for creation a divine dissatisfaction (*arkestha*) that would extend the range of its goodness to originally non-existent beings.

Is there a hint here of necessity, a return to ideas whose natural home might have been Origenism or one or another form of Platonism? One could speculate here and surmise that John would urge that goodness "naturally" (i.e., freely and without compulsion) seeks objects with which to share itself. Such would be consistent with John's claims elsewhere that the world was created in freedom.[23] But what is more crucial to the present discussion is the claim that the created world has a vital connection with God's own reality. That claim is bolstered elsewhere by references to God's penetration of all that has been made. Our second chapter made special note of important biblical texts in Book One, especially in the fourth and eighth chapters. Chapter 4 raises the issue in the form of a question:

> And, again, how can the principle be maintained that God *permeates and fills all things*, as Scripture says: "Do I not fill heaven and earth, saith the Lord"? *For it is impossible for one body to permeate others without dividing and being divided, without being blended and contrasted*, just as when a number of liquids are mixed together and blended.[24]

The larger context surrounding these words deals with the final unknowability of God's essence. God's ability to permeate and fill all is taken as one more instance of that unknowable essence, because there is no question in John's presentation that God does not pervade all or that that permeation somehow alters God's essential character.

---

22. Joh.D. *OF* II.2.1–6 (trans. Chase, 205; emphasis added).

23. See chap. 2 above, especially the section on "Apophasis and the Limits of Creation."

24. Joh.D. *OF* I.4.9–13. (trans. Chase, 171; emphasis added).

The same point is made in chapter 8 of Book One where John affirms God as the maker of all things who providentially sustains them and goes on to speak of God as "filling all things, contained by nothing, but Himself containing all things . . . pervading all substances without being defiled . . ."[25] The same chapter can speak further specifically of the Holy Spirit as one ". . . who deifies but is not deified; who fills but is not filled; who is shared in but does not share; who sanctifies but is not sanctified . . . and is *participated in by all creation*."[26] In each case, whether in creation or in the restoration of creation, God is in some way united with the world in a fashion that is absolutely crucial for creaturely existence but that leaves the divine nature unaltered. Just as the sun shines down on the earth but seemingly remains unaffected by what transpires on the surface of the earth, so God creates and sustains creation but in a unilateral manner that precludes reciprocal influence.[27]

God's relationship to humanity provides a special case in the union between God and the world. Whereas the providential ordering of the world is virtually constant, God's connection with humans has a quality that admits of greater and more "personal" involvement. Humanity was created to live in God's presence with a degree of awareness and intimacy denied to other creatures. Chapter 11 of Book Two notes the duality of body and mind that human existence enshrines: "For while in man's body, he dwelt in this most sacred and beautiful place [Eden] . . . spiritually, he resided in a loftier and far more beautiful place. There he had the indwelling God as a dwelling place and wore him as a glorious garment."[28] This spiritual dwelling, which was at the same time an indwelling, John allegorically indentifies as the tree of life.[29] In the same chapter of Book Two, he has God speak to humanity thus:

> "Of every tree of paradise thou shalt eat," meaning, I think, By means of all created things be thou drawn to Me, their Creator, and from them reap the one fruit which is Myself, who am the true life; let all things be fruitful life to thee and *make participation in Me to be the substance of thine own existence*; for thus thou shalt be immortal.[30]

---

25. Joh.D. *OF* I.8.11–13 (trans. Chase, 177).
26. Joh.D. *OF* I.8.179–83 (trans. Chase, 183–84; emphasis added).
27. Joh.D. *OF* I.10.11–16 (trans. Chase, 191).
28. Joh.D. *OF* II.11.44–49 (trans. Chase, 232).
29. Joh.D. *OF* II.11.49–51 (trans. Chase, 232).
30. Joh.D. *OF* II.11.78–82 (trans. Chase, 233; emphasis added).

John avoids, in this particular context, the inherited language about humanity as reflecting God's image and likeness and speaks instead of human personhood receiving its fulfillment in union with divine being. If John had spoken here of humanity in terms of "image" or "icon," it would seem clear that that quality, whatever else it might mean, could not have been constructed as a quality "possessed" apart from a true connection with God such as prevailed before the Fall.[31] It is to humanity's damaged relationship that we will now turn.

The Loss of Union with God through the Fall

In chapter 4 of Book Four of *The Orthodox Faith*, John Damascene does use the traditional image/likeness language but in the context of Christ's redemptive work. In a fashion common among the Greek Fathers, he distinguishes image from likeness, thereby indicating what a loss of each would entail:

> For [the Son of God] has made [humanity] to his own image, understanding and free, and to his own likeness, that is to say, as perfect in virtues as it was possible for human nature to be, for these virtues are, as it were, characteristics of the divine nature—freedom from care and annoyance, integrity, goodness, wisdom, justice, freedom from all vice. Thus, he puts man in communion with himself and through this communion with himself raised him to incorruptibility, "for he created man incorruptible."[32]

Note the link between the immortality and the communion. Lacking the communion, the immortality ceases to exist. The Fall entails the virtual disappearance of the image.:

> But, since by transgressing the commandment we obscured and canceled out the characteristics of the divine image, we were given over to evil and stripped of the divine communion . . . Then, since we had been removed from life, we fell subject to the destruction of death.[33]

The stage is now set for redemption because the participation, the communion, that was foundational to life in the Garden had been shattered by disobedience. By turning away from the true and only source of life, we

---

31. See the outstanding article by Zizioulas, "Human Capacity," 28, 401–48; reprinted in Zizioulas, *Communion and Otherness*, 206–49.

32. Joh.D. *OF* IV.4.10–16 (trans. Chase, 337).

33. Joh.D. *OF* IV.4.16–20 (trans. Chase, 337–38).

embraced death instead. The next "chapter" in the human drama needed to be that of the image reclaimed and restored.

Union Regained through Christ's Redemption

The restoration of the lost image takes place, for John Damascene, in the context of an exchange. In our previous chapter, much was said about the logic of John's Christology requiring that Christ take on the limitations of human experience in order to heal what had been damaged by sin and death. Christ did not, of course, live through every single thing that humans might undergo—he never endured childbirth or a kidney transplant, shall we say—but a broad range of human limitations, from ordinary hunger and fatigue to acute pain and finally death, was part of his incarnate life. Such, according to John's soteriological perspective, was required in order that our loss might be recovered. An exchange needed to take place so that we might receive once again what had originally been given to us:

> But, since He had shared with us what was better and we had not kept it, He now takes His share of what is worse, of our nature I mean to say, that through Himself and in Himself He may restore was to His image and what was to His likeness, while also teaching us the virtuous way of life which He has made easy of ascent for us through Him, and that, having become the first fruits of our resurrection, He may by the communication of life free us from death and restore the useless and worn-out vessel, and so that, having called us to the knowledge of God, He may redeem us from the tyranny of the Devil and by patience and humility teach us to overthrow the tyrant.[34]

The restoration of the image entailed assumption of full humanity, the transformation of the humanity assumed, and the communication of that transformed humanity.

John Damascene, however, offers no suggestion that Christ took on a generalized transpersonal humanity that, as transformed, is secretly at work in the redemption of each individual regardless of any conscious relationship to Christ. A quasi-physical understanding of salvation does not describe the change that becomes possible through some kind of participation in the deified humanity of Christ. The link between the fallen humanity of individual persons and the saving humanity of the Word is set forth rather in sacramental terms.

---

34 Joh.D. *OF* IV.4.20–28 (trans. Chase, 338).

The primary sacrament, at least in terms of the sequence of appropriation of the Christian life, is of course baptism. By way of explaining why the only-begotten Son also needed to be born of a mother, John says,

> For this very reason, that He shared flesh and blood along with us and then, also, that we were made sons of God through Him by being adopted through baptism, He who is by nature Son of God has become first-born among us who have by adoption and grace become sons of God and are accounted His brethren.[35]

The link between fallen humanity and the divine Christ is that of baptismal grace, whereby what is lacking by nature is received through adoption. Baptism, in which both water and the Spirit are active, purifies with these two elements the two-part character of those who are baptized:

> For since man is twofold, being of body and soul, the purification [God] gave us is also twofold, renewing in us what is to His image and likeness and the water by grace of the Spirit purifying the body from sin and delivering it from destruction—the water completing the figure of death and the Spirit producing the guarantee of life.[36]

The twin foes, sin and death, are conquered by the Spirit-endowed water of baptism. The sacrament of initiation becomes thereby the conduit whereby the deified humanity of Christ, a humanity that was hypostatized in the individual person of the incarnate Logos, can be passed on to the humanity of other individual persons. The participation in the person of Christ is a sacramental participation that moves on a different plane from that of Christ embodying a generalized humanity that somehow automatically confers transfiguration on the whole race that is united to it as particulars united to the ideal form in which they participate.

Baptismal grace, however, might still suggest a quasi-physical connection between Christ and baptized humanity whereby the latter are automatically incorporated into Christ by virtue of the sacramental action. But John does not neglect the dimension of faith without which, for him, all else is in vain. In chapter 11 of Book Four, where he proclaims the centrality of the cross, he asserts: "*Without faith it is impossible to be saved*, since by faith all things endure, both human and spiritual."[37] Faith is extolled as crucial to salvation in a way that eliminates a merely passive acceptance of union with Christ. One is reminded of the discussion of our last chapter in which

---

35. Joh.D. *OF* IV.8.12–16 (trans. Chase, 343).
36. Joh.D. *OF* IV.9.36–42 (trans. Chase, 345).
37. Joh.D. *OF* IV.9.13–14 (trans. Chase, 349; emphasis added).

the humanity of Christ was seen as possessing its own will and action and cooperating in the saving work of the divine will.

In the present context, the cruciality of Christ's assuming a human will surfaces because what the will requires is deifying or sanctifying, not effacing. What we are left with is neither Pelagianism nor fatalism. The will sanctified by the grace of baptism is enabled to act in accord with the divine will. Unlike the will joined in hypostatic union to the Logos, however, it is susceptible to being either more or less and can potentially fall away altogether. Herein lies an instance where the difference between participation and *perichoresis* becomes visible. Participation entails a *hypostasis* distinct from that of the Word to which it is joined. For that reason, the relationship established has an inconstancy that the Christ of Chalcedon (as interpreted by the post-Chalcedonian councils) could never have.

The relation of baptism to eucharistic communion is that of birth to food: baptism brings spiritual rebirth; communion sustains that birth. In both cases, a spiritual component is compounded with a physical one in recognition of the duality of human nature:

> Now, since this Adam is spiritual, it was necessary that there be a spiritual birth and also a spiritual food. But since we are individuals of a twofold nature and compounded, it is necessary that the birth also be of a twofold nature and the food be compounded. Hence, the birth was given us by water and the Spirit, by holy baptism, I mean, while the food was the Bread of Life itself, our Lord Jesus Christ who had come down from heaven.[38]

The joining of spiritual and physical is crucial. In communion, the elements are the actual body and blood that, in the Incarnation, were joined to the Godhead. How this is possible is a mystery fundamentally pneumatological. Should one inquire into how such a thing could be, John would reply: "Let it suffice for you to hear that it is done through the Holy Spirit, just as it was through the Holy Spirit that the Lord made flesh subsist for Himself and in Himself from the blessed Mother of God."[39] To those who see in the bread and wine mere symbols of what they would represent, John has these words:

> The bread and wine are not a figure of the body and blood of Christ—God forbid!—but the actual deified body of the Lord, because the Lord Himself said, "This is my body"; not a "figure

---

38. Joh.D. *OF* IV.13.40–45 (trans. Chase, 355).
39. Joh.D. *OF* IV,13.97–99 (trans. Chase, 358).

of my body" but "my body," and not "a figure of my blood" but "my blood."[40]

The realism underlying such a conception is a working out of the logic of participation whereby Christ's sanctified humanity must in some way become available to the rest of humanity.

That deified humanity bears essentially the same relationship to baptized humanity that the divine nature of Christ bears to his human nature; it changes the other without itself being changed. And the change it effects does not alter the essential structure of the lesser party; rather, it enhances and fulfills it. As noted above, the hypostatic union has its own unique features that mark the difference between *perichoresis* and participation. At the same time, those features give a strong analogical connection. In each case, the realities brought together remain distinct and without confusion.

Nevertheless, taking Christ's body into our body changes us in a fundamental way: a union between the two is established that allows us to be, in a very real sense, one with Christ: "When we are purified by it [the Lord's body], we become one with the body of the Lord and with His Spirit, and we become the body of Christ."[41] At the same time, Christ's own body remains what it was:

> It is Christ's body and blood entering into the composition of our soul and body without being consumed, without being corrupted, without passing into the privy [sic!]—God forbid!—but into our substance for our substance, a bulwark against every sort of harm and a purifier for all uncleanliness—as if he were to take unadulterated gold and purify it by the discerning fire, so that in the life to come we shall not be condemned with the world.[42]

The duality of the relationship between Christ and the baptized person has about it, then, the element of identity and difference that is at the root of *perichoresis*. Union without confusion is the structural analogue that at the same time provides space for significant differences.

These differences are recognized in the language that John chooses to set forth the relationship established sacramentally. Even though the vocabulary of mutual indwelling is available for use, John employs words like participation and communion to speak of the connection brought about by the consecrated bread and wine:

40. Joh.D. *OF* IV.13.114–117 (trans. Chase, 358).
41. Joh.D. *OF* IV.13.153–154 (trans. Chase, 360).
42. Joh.D. *OF* IV.13.143–151 (trans. Chase, 360).

> It is called *participation* [*metalapsis*] because through it we participate [*metalambanomen*] in the divinity of Jesus. It is also called *communion* [*koinonia*], and is truly so, because of our having communion through it with Christ and partaking [*metechein*] both of his flesh and his divinity, and because through it we have communion with and are united to one another. For, since we partake of one bread, we all become one body of Christ and one blood and members of one another and are accounted of the same body with Christ.[43]

Such language allows us to claim identity with Christ without either being swallowed up by his divinity or absorbing him in our humanity. It also allows scope for an ecclesiological extension of that relationship by pointing to a double reality: those who are united to Christ are thereby united to each other as well. We become one with Christ's own body, not only in its individual historical dimension but in its ecclesiological and eschatological dimensions also. In each case, identity and difference are preserved.

Final Union with God in the Life to Come

The loss of the image and likeness in the Garden was at the same time a loss of immortality and a partaking (a participation in) sin and corruption. Our previous section indicated the role of baptism in the removal of sin and death. It also exhibited the connection between communion and the restoration of the image. But the fact remains that the baptized person must still face corruption and death and, with the latter, the separation of body and soul. In response to the unavoidable question raised by death, John Damascene points to the resurrection, which he sees not only as a bringing back together of body and soul but also as a union connecting the soul with a transformed body beyond the reach of decay and dissolution. He says, "And it is plain that the resurrection of the Lord was uniting of a soul with an incorrupted body . . ." and goes on to quote the New Testament at length to the effect that the natural body will be turned into a spiritual body.[44]

On this basis, John is able to affirm the ultimate resurrection of all believers who, through their union with the exalted Christ, will participate in the same glorification: "And so, with our souls again united to our bodies, which will become incorrupt and put off corruption, we shall rise again

---

43. Joh.D. *OF* IV.13.167–172 (trans. Chase, 361).

44. Joh.D. *OF* IV.13.83–91 (trans. Chase, 404). The following New Testament passages are quoted or alluded to: 1 Cor 15:16, 17, 20; Col 1:18; 1 Thess. 4:13; John 2:19, 21; Luke 24:39, 40; John 20:27.

and stand before the terrible judgment seat of Christ."⁴⁵ It is in the final scene that our restored image and deified flesh will manifest themselves and the instability inherent in our present experience of participation will be removed. The final state will move participation closer to the permanency of mutual indwelling.

---

45. Joh.D. *OF* IV.27.123–25 (trans. Chase, 406).

Epilogue

THE PRECEDING CHAPTERS HAVE ATTEMPTED TO TRACE JOHN OF Damascus's use of *perichoresis* throughout his *Exact Exposition of the Orthodox Faith* and take the measure of its range of application in relation to John's understanding of God, Christ, and salvation. Even though the language of mutual indwelling takes on different shape and coloring as it moves through each of these doctrines, it nevertheless reveals a constant deep structure in which identity and difference form the basic elements. This is not to say that *perichoresis* is a certain "something" that can stand apart from particular contexts; rather, it is to affirm that there is a definite commonality in the various usages to which the term is put.

Perichoresis, in John's thought, represents a summing up of centuries of reflection and controversy. With regard to the Trinity, it offers a retrospective rationale for the classical Cappadocian formulations, a rationale that was shaped mainly by the subsequent christological debates. The unity without confusion that lies at the heart of Chalcedonian Christology was refined by later councils aided by theologians of the stature of Maximus the Confessor. John employed that developed form in the service of explicating the doctrine of the Trinity. By making use of a Chalcedonian form of reasoning, he was able to give added cogency to the affirmation of *mia ousia, treis hypostaseis*.

The Chalcedonian basis of *perichoresis* in relation to Christology is manifestly obvious. Almost every reference to mutual indwelling in John Damascene's work is accompanied by the qualification, often supported by the Chalcedonian adverbs, that the relationship of two natures in one person entails neither separation nor confusion. Such is true with the Trinitarian references to mutual indwelling as well; but in this case, the Chalcedonian logic comes in from the outside, as it were, to bolster and give added clarity to a doctrine that was originally formulated without a clear notion of *perichoresis*. The doctrine of Christ, on the other hand, finds a clear basis for at least a rudimentary expression of mutual indwelling at the very outset in the formulation of Chalcedon. That these formulations needed further refining is amply demonstrated by the subsequent controversies and the clarifications represented by *enhypostasia*, two wills and operations, and so on. But the foundation had been laid by the Fourth Council, and later developments clearly built on that.

If the Chalcedonian link with *perichoresis* is manifestly clear, less obvious perhaps but equally important is the reciprocal move whereby matters worked out in relation to the Trinity provide resources for solving christological problems and give *perichoresis* firmer footing in relation to Christ. By positing one will and operation, and not three, for the *hypostaseis* of the Trinity and locating that oneness in the common nature and not in the separate "persons," a rationale was provided for doing the same with the two natures of Christ. Each nature is allowed to have its own will and operation without requiring Christ to have two persons. The personalizing character of the Logos can lay claim to two wills and two operations without its personhood being divided. *Perichoresis* holds the two sides together in the hypostatic union whereby the human and divine natures of the incarnate Logos mutually indwell or interpenetrate each other.

So the respective uses of *perichoresis* in the Trinity and the Incarnation are linked in mutually supportive ways. The case for using mutual indwelling in relation to John's understanding of salvation, however, is less clear because *perichoresis* invariably refers to constancy in the union of the realities so united that does not encompass the fluctuation of faith and obedience represented by human response to God. Here, the language of participation and communion, a language that allows for the possibility of flux, is more fitting and is indeed that which John uses in connection with salvation. What is true of God and of Christ by nature becomes in an appropriate measure available to humanity by grace. The deified humanity of Christ becomes the vehicle through which Christ's deity can be savingly offered. That humanity becomes present through baptism and the Lord's supper. Baptism allows one to enter into Christ's death and thereby die to one's sinful nature; the eucharist feeds one with that which will restore and strengthen the image of God. Each does so by enabling one to participate in God through Christ in the Spirit. That participation is, by analogy, a reduced version of mutual indwelling in which the human personality is preserved and enhanced and, yet, within the measure of faith present, controlled by the divine reality in which it participates.

I have made a strenuous attempt to present *perichoresis* as a major advance in terminological clarification whereby God and Christ (and by contrast salvation) can be seen in terms of identity and difference in more illuminating and persuasive ways. A major part of that clarification is the demonstration that *perichoresis* represents a summing up of a whole series of terminological advances between the fourth and the eighth centuries, a summing up that reveals an expanding capacity to gather up new insights and make them part of its meaning. By setting forth the intellectual and spiritual bases for John Damascene's use of *perichoresis* and exhibiting its uses in terms of three key doctrines, I hope I have made a serious contribution of my own to the task of theological clarification.

Clarification in relation to *perichoresis* is clearly urgent, given the renewed interest in Trinitarianism and the unending concern to find fitting ways of setting forth Christ's complex relation both to God and to creation. Discussion in recent years has expanded these two areas of concern to include the ecclesial and social realms. Without suggesting that John's own usages preclude this kind of expansion, a word of caution might nevertheless be necessary. By carefully restricting mutual-indwelling language to the Trinity and the Incarnation, John not only turned to the language of participation to set forth other kinds of relationship but provided a clear rationale for us to do the same.

But there are examples in John of Damascus's own deployment of perichoretic issues that reveal creative advances in what might appear as wider territory and thereby provide a warrant for us to do likewise. His writings in support of icons, for instance, take a debate that could have foundered in the morass of popular piety and reveal that, at its very heart, it involves profound christological concerns.[1] In our day, perhaps there are those who can grasp the depths of *perichoresis* in terms of the classical Christian doctrines and go on to probe its implications for enlarged areas of theological interest. It would be gratifying to think that the ground-clearing attempted here could provide a major starting point.

---

1. See the Greek text of *Contra imaginum calumiatores orationes tres* in Kotter, *Schriften*, vol. 3. See also translations by Anderson of St. John of Damascus, *On the Divine Images*; and by Louth of John of Damascus, *Three Treatises*. The literature referred to in note 4 of chapter 3 above is worth consulting.

Bibliography

Ables, Scott. "The Anti-Monophysite Trinitarian Christology of John of Damascus." Paper presented at the annual meeting of the North American Patristics Society, Chicago, Illinois, May 30, 2010.

Agoras, Constantin. "L'Anthropolgie Theologique de Jean Zizioulas." *Contacts* N.S. 41 (1989) 6–23.

Allen, Diogenes. *Philosophy for Understanding Theology*. Atlanta: John Knox, 1985.

Altaner, Berthold. *Patrologie*. Freiburg: Herder, 1951.

Anastos, Thomas Leo. "Essence, Energies and Hypostasis: An Epistemological Analysis of the Eastern Orthodox Model of God." PhD diss., Yale University, 1986.

Anatolios, Khalid. *Retrieving Nicea: The Development and Meaning of Trinitarian Doctrine*. Grand Rapids: Baker Academic, 2011.

Armstrong, A. H., ed. *The Cambridge History of Later Greek and Early Medieval Philosophy*. Cambridge: Cambridge University Press, 1967.

———. *An Introduction to Ancient Philosophy*. 4th ed. London: Methuen, 1965.

Armstrong, A. H., and R. A. Markus. *Christian Thought and Greek Philosophy*. London: Darton, Longman and Todd, 1960.

Athanasius, Saint, Patriarch of Alexandria. *Select Works and Letters*. Vol. 4 of *Nicene and Post-Nicene Fathers of the Christian Church*, Second Series. Edited by Philip Schaff and Henry Wace. Reprint, Grand Rapids: Eerdmans, 1978.

Ayres, Lewis. *Nicaea and Its Legacy: An Approach to Fourth-Century Trinitarian Theology*. Oxford: Oxford University Press, 2006.

Baillie, D. M. *God Was in Christ*. New York: Scribner's, 1948.

Balas, David L. *METOUSIA THEOU: Man's Participation in God's Perfections according to St. Gregory of Nyssa*. Rome: Libreria Herder, 1966.

Balthasar, Hans Urs von. *Liturgie Cosmique, Maxime le Confesseur*. Translated (from German) by L. Lhaumet and H.-A. Pretout. Paris: Aubier, 1947.

Barth, Karl. *Church Dogmatics*. Vol. I/1. Translated by G. T. Thomson. Edinburgh: T. & T. Clark, 1936.

Basil, Saint, Bishop of Caesarea. *Letters and Select Works*. Vol. 8 of *Nicence and Post-Nicene Fathers of the Christian Church*, Second Series. Edited by Philip Schaff and Henry Wace. Reprint, Grand Rapids: Eerdmans, 1978.

———. *On the Holy Spirit*. Translated by David Anderson. Crestwood, NY: St. Vladimir's Seminary Press, 1980.

Beeley, Christopher. *The Unity of Christ: Continuity and Conflict in Patristic Tradition*. New Haven: Yale University Press, 2012.

Bibliography

Berthold, George C., trans. and ed. *Maximus Confessor, Selected Writings*. Classics of Western Spirituality. New York: Paulist, 1985.

Bigg, C. *The Christian Platonists of Alexandria*. Oxford: Clarendon, 1913.

Bondi, Roberta C. "Immutability." In *Westminster Dictionary of Christian Theology*, edited by Alan Richardson and John Bowden, 288. Philadelphia: Westminster, 1983.

Bouthier, Michel. *Christianity according to Paul*. Studies in Biblical Theology 49. London: SCM, 1966.

Brown, Peter. *The World of Late Antiquity, AD 150–750*. London: Thames and Hudson, 1971.

Burnaby, John, trans. and ed. *Augustine: Later Works*. Library of Christian Classics 8. Philadelphia: Westminster, 1955.

Cabasilas, Nicholas. *The Life in Christ*. Translated by Carmino deCatanzaro. Crestwood, NY: St. Vladimir's Seminary Press, 1974.

Campenhausen, Hans von. *The Fathers of the Greek Church*. Translated by L. A. Garrard. London: A. & C. Black, 1963.

Chadwick, Henry. "Eucharist and Christology in the Nestorian Controversy." *Journal of Theological Studies* N.S. 2 (1951) 145–64.

Chesnut [Bondi], Roberta C. *Three Monophysite Christologies: Severus of Antioch, Philoxenus of Mabbug, and Jacob of Sarug*. Oxford: Oxford University Press, 1976.

———. "The Two Prosopa in Nestorius' Bazaar of Heraclides." *Journal of Theological Studies* N.S. 29 (1978) 392–409.

Chitty, Derwas. *The Desert a City*. Crestwood, NY: St. Vladimir's Seminary Press, n.d.

Coakley, Sarah, ed. *Re-thinking Gregory of Nyssa*. Oxford: Blackwell, 2003.

Cochrane, Charles N. *Christianity and Classical Culture: A Study of Thought and Action from Augustus to Augustine*. Oxford: Clarendon, 1940.

Conticello, Vassa S. "Pseudo-Cyril's 'De Ss. Trinitate': A Compilation of Joseph the Philosopher." *Orientalia Christiana Periodica* 61 (1995) 117–29.

Cornford, F. M. *Plato's Theory of Knowledge*. Cambridge: Cambridge University Press, 1935.

Crisp, Oliver D. *Divinity and Humanity: The Incarnation Reconsidered*. Cambridge: Cambridge University Press, 2007.

Cross, Richard. "Perichoresis, Deification, and Christological Predication in John of Damascus." *Medieval Studies* 62 (2000) 69–124.

Cunliffe-Jones, Hubert, ed. *A History of Christian Doctrine*. Philadelphia: Fortress, 1980.

Cunningham, F. L. B. *The Indwelling of the Trinity*. Dubuque, IA: Priory, 1955.

Deneffe, August. "Perichoresis, Circumincessio, Circumincessio, Ein Terminologische Untersuchung." *Zeitschrift für Katholische Theologie* 47 (1923) 497–532.

Evans, David Beecher. *Leontius of Byzantium: An Origenist Christology*. Washington, DC: Dumbarton Oaks Center for Byzantine Studies, 1970.

Every, George. "The Study of Eastern Orthodoxy: Hesychasm." *Religion* 9 (1979) 73–91.

Fairbairn, Donald. *Grace and Christology in the Early Church*. Oxford: Oxford University Press, 2006.

Florovsky, Georges. *Aspects of Church History*. Collected Works of Georges Florovsky 4. Belmont, MA: Nordlund, 1975.

———. *Bible, Church, Tradition: An Eastern Orthodox View*. Collected Works of Georges Florovsky 1. Belmont, MA: Nordlund, 1972.

---. *The Byzantine Ascetic and Spiritual Fathers*. Edited by Richard S. Haugh. Translated by Raymond Miller et al. Collected Works of Georges Florovsky 10. Vaduz: Buchervertreibsanstalt, 1987.

---. *The Byzantine Fathers of the Fifth Century*. Edited by Richard S. Haugh. Translated by Raymond Miller et al. Collected Works of Georges Florovsky 8. Vaduz: Buchervertreibsanstalt, 1987.

---. *The Byzantine Fathers of the Sixth to Eighth Century*. Edited by Richard S. Haugh. Translated by Raymond Miller et al. Collected Works of Georges Florovsky 9. Vaduz: Buchervertreibsanstalt, 1987.

---. *Creation and Redemption*. Collected Works of Georges Florovsky 3. Belmont, MA: Nordlund, 1976.

---. *The Eastern Fathers of the Fourth Century*. Edited by Richard S. Haugh. Translated by Catherine Edmunds. Collected Works of Georges Florovsky 7. Vaduz: Buchervertreibsanstalt, 1987.

Fortman, Edmund J. *The Triune God: A Historical Study of the Doctrine of the Trinity*. Grand Rapids: Baker, 1972.

Frend, W. H. C. *The Rise of Christianity*. Philadelphia: Fortress, 1984.

---. *The Rise of the Monophysite Movement*. Cambridge: Cambridge University Press, 1972.

Fries, Paul R., and Tiran Nersoyan, eds. *Christ in East and West*. Macon, GA: Mercer University Press, 1987.

Gifford, James D., Jr. *Perichoretic Salvation: The Believer's Union with Christ as a Third Type of Perichoresis*. Eugene, OR: Wipf and Stock, 2011.

Gregg, Robert C., and Dennis E. Groh. "The Centrality of Soteriology in Early Arianism." *Anglican Theological Review* 59 (1977) 266–78.

---. *Early Arianism—A View of Salvation*. Philadelphia: Westminster, 1981.

Gregory, of Nyssa, Saint. *Dogmatic Treatises, etc.* Vol. 5 of *Nicene and Post-Nicene Fathers of the Christian Church*, Second Series. Edited by Philip Schaff and Henry Wace. Reprint, Grand Rapids: Eerdmans, 1979.

Gregory, of Nazianzus, Saint (and Cyril of Jerusalem). *S. Cyril of Jerusalem. S. Gregory Nazianzen*. Vol. 7 of *Nicene and Post-Nicene Fathers of the Christian Church*, Second Series. Edited by Philip Schaff and Henry Wace. Reprint, Grand Rapids: Eerdmans, 1978.

Grillmeier, Aloys. *Christ in the Christian Tradition*. Vol. 1, *From the Apostolic Age to Chalcedon (451)*. Translated by John Bowden. Atlanta: John Knox, 1975.

---. *Christ in the Christian Tradition*. Vol. 2/1, *From Chalcedon to Justinian I*. Translated by Pauline Allen and John Cawte. Atlanta: John Knox, 1987.

Grillmeier, Aloys, and Heinrich Badt, eds. *Das Konzil von Chalkedon: Geschichte und Gegenwart*. 3 vols. Würzburg: Echter, 1951–1954.

Gruenler, Royce Gordon. *The Trinity in the Gospel of John: A Thematic Commentary on the Fourth Gospel*. Grand Rapids: Baker, 1986.

Gundry, Robert. *Soma in Biblical Theology: With Emphasis on Pauline Anthropology*. Grand Rapids: Zondervan, 1987.

Gunton, Colin E. *The One, the Three, and the Many: God, Creation, and the Culture of Modernity*. 1992 Bampton Lectures. Cambridge: Cambridge University Press, 1993.

Guthrie, W. K. C. *The Greek Philosphers: From Thales to Aristotle*. New York: Harper & Row, 1960.

Bibliography

Hamell, Patrick J. *Handbook of Patrology*. Staten Island, NY: Alba House, 1968.

Hardy, Edward Rochie, and Cyril R. Richardson, eds. and trans. *Christology of the Later Fathers*. Library of Christian Classics 3. Philadelphia: Westminster, 1954.

Harnack, Adolf. *History of Dogma*. Vols. 1–8. Translated by Neil Buchanan. 1900. Reprint, New York: Dover, 1961.

———. *What Is Christianity?* Translated by T. B. Saunders. New York: Putnam, 1901.

Harrison, Verna. "Perichoresis in the Greek Fathers." *St. Vladimir's Theological Quarterly* 35 (1991) 53–65.

Hebblethwaite, Brian. *The Incarnation: Collected Essays in Christology*. Cambridge: Cambridge University Press, 1987.

Hurtado, Larry W. *One God, One Lord: Early Christian Devotion and Ancient Jewish Monotheism*. Philadelphia: Fortress, 1988.

Jaeger, Werner. *The Theology of the Greek Philosophers*. Oxford: Clarendon, 1947.

Jean Damascène (S.). *Homilies sur la Nativité et la Dormition*. Edited and translated by Pierre Voulet. Sources Chrétiennes 80. Paris: Cerf, 1961.

Jenson, Robert. *The Triune Identity*. Philadelphia: Fortress, 1982.

John, of Damascus, Saint. *De Fide Orthodoxa, Versions of Burgundio and Cerbanus*. Edited by Eligius M. Buytaert. Franciscan Institutes Publications, Text Series, No. 8. St. Bonaventure, NY: Franciscan Institute, 1955.

———. *On the Divine Images: Three Apologies against Those Who Attack the Holy Images*. Translated by David Anderson. Crestwood, NY: St. Vladimir's Seminary Press, 1980.

———. *Opera*. Vols. 94–96 of *Patrologia graeca*, edited by J.-P. Migne. Paris, 1857–86.

———. *Three Treatises on the Divine Images*. Translated by Andrew Louth. Popular Patristics. Crestwood, NY: St. Vladimir's Seminary Press, 2003.

———. *Writings*. Translated by Frederic H. Chase Jr. Fathers of the Church. New York: Fathers of the Church, 1958.

John of Damascus (and Hilary of Poitiers). *St. Hilary of Poitiers, John of Damascus*. Vol. 9 of *Nicene and Post-Nicene Fathers of the Christian Church*, Second Series. Edited by Philip Schaff and Henry Wace. Reprint, Grand Rapids: Eerdmans, 1989.

Johnson, Aubrey R. *The One and the Many in the Israelite Conception of God*. Cardiff: University of Wales, 1942.

———. *The Vitality of the Individual in the Thought of Ancient Israel*. Cardiff: University of Wales, 1949.

Jugie, M. "Jean Damascène." In *Dictionnaire de Theologie Catholique*, edited by E. Mangenot et al., 8:693–751. Paris: Letouzey and Ane, 1924.

Kaiser, Christopher B. *The Doctrine of God*. Westchester, IL: Crossway, 1982.

Kelly, J. N. D. *Early Christian Creeds*. London: Longman's Green, 1950.

———. *Early Christian Doctrines*. 4th ed. London: A. & C. Black, 1968.

Knight, G. A. F. *A Biblical Approach to the Doctrine of the Trinity*. Edinburgh: Oliver and Boyd, 1953.

Koester, Helmut. "Hypostasis." In *Theological Dictionary of the New Testament*, edited by Gerhard Kittel, translated by Geoffrey W. Bromiley, 8:572–89. Grand Rapids: Eerdmans, 1964–74.

Kotter, Bonifatius, ed. *Die Schriften des Johannes von Damaskos*. Vol. 1, *Institutio Elementararis, Capita Philosphica (Dialectica)*. Berlin: de Gruyter, 1973.

———. *Die Schriften des Johannes von Damaskos*. Vol. 2, *Expositio Fidei*. Berlin: de Gruyter, 1973.

———. *Die Schriften des Johannes von Damaskos*. Vol. 3, *Contra imaginum calumniatores orationes tres*. Berlin: de Gruyter, 1975.

———. *Die Schriften des Johannes von Damaskos*. Vol. 4, *Liber de haerisibus, Opera polemica*. Berlin: de Gruyter, 1988.

———. *Die Schriften des Johannes von Damaskos*. Vol. 5, *Opera homiletica and hagiographica*. Berlin: de Gruyter, 1988.

———. "Johannes von Damaskus." In *Theologische Realenzyklopaedie*, edited by Gerhard Mueller et al., 17:127–32. Berlin: de Gruyter, 1988.

Kotter, P. Bonifaz. *Die Überlieferung der Pege Gnoseos de Hl. Johannes von Damaskos*. Studia Patristica et Byzantina. Ettal: Buch-Kunstverlag, 1959.

Laeuchli, Samuel. *The Serpent and the Dove*. Nashville: Abingdon, 1960.

Lampe, G. W. H. *God as Spirit*. London: SCM, 1983.

———. *A Patristic Greek Lexicon*. Oxford: Clarendon, 1961.

Lawler, Michael G. "Perichoresis: New Theological Wine in an Old Theological Wineskin." *Horizons* 22 (1995) 49–66.

Lebreton, J. *History of the Doctrine of the Trinity from Its Origins to the Council of Nicea*. Translated by Algar Thorold. New York: Benzinger, 1939.

Letham, Robert. *The Holy Trinity: In Scripture, History, Theology, and Worship*. Phillipsburg, NJ: P&R, 2004.

Liddell, Henry George, and Robert Scott. *An Intermediate Greek-English Lexicon*. Oxford: Clarendon, 1889.

Lloyd, G. E. R. *Aristotle: The Growth and Structure of His Thought*. Cambridge: Cambridge University Press, 1968.

Lossky, Vladimir. *In the Image and Likeness of God*. Edited by John H. Erickson and Thomas E. Bird. Crestwood, NY: St. Vladimir's Seminary Press, 1974.

———. *The Mystical Theology of the Eastern Church*. Translated by members of the Fellowship of St. Alban and St. Sergius. Cambridge: James Clarke, 1957.

———. *The Vision of God*. Translated by Asheleigh Moorhouse. Crestwood, NY: St. Vladimir's Seminary Press, 1963.

Louth, Andrew. *The Origins of the Christian Mystical Tradition from Plato to Denys*. Oxford: Clarendon, 1981.

———. *St. John Damascene: Tradition and Originality in Byzantine Theology*. Oxford Early Christian Studies. Oxford: Oxford University Press, 2001.

Macmurray, John. *Persons in Relation*. Reprint, Atlantic Highlands, NJ: Humanities, 1979.

———. *The Self as Agent*. Reprint, Atlantic Highlands, NJ: Humanities, 1978.

Mask, E. Jeffrey. "The Doctrine of the Trinity in the Work of Karl Barth, Leonard Hodgson, and Jürgen Moltmann." Paper presented to Southeastern meeting of the American Academy of Religion, 1985.

McGrath, Alister E. *Understanding the Trinity*. Grand Rapids: Zondervan, 1988.

Meyendorff, John. *Byzantine Theology: Historical Trends and Doctrinal Themes*. London: Mowbrays, 1974.

———. *Christ in Eastern Christian Thought*. Crestwood, NY: St. Vladimir's Seminary Press, 1975.

———. *A Study in Gregory Palamas*. London: Faith, 1964.

Moltmann, Jürgen. *The Crucified God*. Translated by R. A. Wilson and John Bowden. New York: Harper & Row, 1974.

———. *The Trinity and the Kingdom*. Translated by Margaret Kohl. San Francisco: Harper & Row, 1981.
Morris, Thomas V. *The Logic of God Incarnate*. Ithaca: Cornell University Press, 1986.
Muller, Richard A. *Dictionary of Latin and Greek Theological Terms*. Grand Rapids: Baker, 1985.
Newman, John Henry. *The Arians of the Fourth Century*. 1833. Reprint, Eugene, OR: Wipf and Stock, 1996.
Norris, Richard A., ed. and trans. *The Christological Controversy*. Philadelphia: Fortress, 1980.
———. *God and World in Early Christian Theology*. New York: Seabury, 1965.
Osborn, Eric. *The Beginning of Christian Philosophy*. Cambridge: Cambridge University Press, 1981.
Osthathios, Mar Gregorios. *Theology of a Classless Society*. Maryknoll, NY: Orbis, 1980.
Otto, Randall E. "The Use and Abuse of Perichoresis in Recent Theology." *Scottish Journal of Theology* 54 (2001) 366–84.
Payne, Robert. *The Holy Fire: The Story of the Fathers of the Eastern Church*. New York: Harper, 1957.
Pelikan, Jaroslav. *The Christian Tradition*. 5 vols. Chicago: University of Chicago Press, 1971–88.
Prestige, G. L. *Fathers and Heretics*. London: SPCK, 1948.
———. *God in Patristic Thought*. London: SPCK, 1952.
Pseudo-Dionysius the Areopagite. *The Divine Names and the Mystical Theology*. Translated by C. E. Rolt. London: SPCK, 1940.
Quasten, Johannes. *Patrology*. Vols. 1–3. 1950–1960. Reprint, Westminster, MD: Christian Classics, 1983.
Radde-Gallwitz, Andrew. *Basil of Caesarea, Gregory of Nyssa, and the Transformation of Divine Simplicity*. Oxford: Oxford University Press, 2009.
Rawlinson, A. E. J., ed. *Essays on the Trinity and the Incarnation*. London: Longman's, Green, 1928.
Richardson, Cyril C. *The Doctrine of the Trinity*. Nashville: Abingdon, 1958.
Richter, Gerhard. *Die Dialektik des Johannes von Damaskos, Eine Untersuchung des Textes nach seinen Quellen und Seine Bedeutung*. 10 Heft. Ettal: Buch-Kunstverlag, 1964.
Ross, W. D. *Aristotle*. London: Methuen, 1956.
———. *Plato's Theory of Ideas*. Oxford: Clarendon, 1953.
Rozemond, Keetje. *La Christologie de Saint Jean Damascene*. Studia Patristica et Byzantina. 8 Heft. Ettal: Buch-Kunstverlag, 1959.
Rusch, William G., ed. and trans. *The Trinitarian Controversy*. Philadelphia: Fortress, 1980.
Sambursky, S. *The Physical World of the Greeks*. Translated by Merton Dagut. New York: Macmillan, 1956.
———. *Physics of the Stoics*. London: Routledge and Kegan Paul, 1959.
Sayers, Dorothy L. *The Mind of the Maker*. London: Methuen, 1941.
Schleiermacher, Friedrich. *The Christian Faith*. Translation edited by H. R. Mackintosh and J. S. Stewart. Edinburgh: T. & T. Clark, 1928.
Schmidt, M. A. *Gottheit un Trinitaet* (Phil. St. 7). Basel: Verlag fuer recht und Gesellschaft, 1956.

Sellers, R. V. *The Council of Chalcedon: A Historical and Doctrinal Survey*. London: SPCK, 1953.

———. *Two Ancient Christologies*. London: SPCK, 1954.

Sherrard, Philip. "Christian Theology and the Eclipse of Man." *Sobornost* 7, no. 3 (1976) 166–79.

———. "The Christian Understanding of Man." *Sobornost* 7, no. 5 (1977) 329–43.

Singh, Surjit. *Christology and Personality*. Philadelphia: Westminster, 1961.

———. *A Philosophy of Integral Relation (Samyagdarsana)*. Madras: Christian Literature Society, n.d.

Smedes, Lewis B. *Union with Christ: A Biblical View of New Life in Christ*. Grand Rapids: Eerdmans, 1970.

Spidlik, Tomas. *The Spirituality of the Christian East: A Systematic Handbook*. Kalamazoo, MI: Cistercian, 1986.

Staniloae, Dumitru. *Theology and the Church*. Crestwood, NY: St. Vladimir's Seminary Press, 1980.

Stead, Christopher. *Divine Substance*. Oxford: Clarendon, 1977.

Stevenson, J., ed. *Creeds, Councils and Controversies*. London: SPCK, 1966.

Stewart, James S. *A Man in Christ: The Vital Elements of St. Paul's Religion*. Grand Rapids: Baker, 1974.

Studer, Basilius. *Die Theologische Arbeitsweise des Johannes von Damaskos*. Studia Patristica et Byzantina. 2 Heft. Ettal: Buch-Kunstverlag, 1956.

Sykes, S. W., and J. P. Clayton, eds. *Christ, Faith, and History*. Cambridge Studies in Christology. Cambridge: Cambridge University Press, 1972.

Thompson, Marianne Meye. *The Humanity of Jesus in the Fourth Gospel*. Philadelphia: Fortress, 1988.

Thunberg, Lars. *Man and the Cosmos: The Vision of Maximus the Confessor*. Crestwood, NY: St. Vladimir's Seminary Press, 1985.

———. *Microcosm and Mediator: The Theological Anthropology of Maximus the Confessor*. Lund: Gleerup, 1965.

Toon, Peter, and James D. Spiceland, eds. *One God in Trinity*. Westchester, IL: Cornerstone, 1980.

Torrance, Thomas F. *The Christian Doctrine of God: One Being, Three Persons*. Edinburgh: T. & T. Clark, 1996.

———. *Incarnation: The Person and Life of Christ*. Downers Grove, IL: IVP Academic, 2008.

———. *Theology in Reconciliation: Essays towards Evangelical and Catholic Unity in East and West*. Grand Rapids: Eerdmans, 1975.

———. "Toward an Ecumenical Consensus on the Trinity." *Theologische Zeitschrift* 31 (1975) 337–50.

———. *The Trinitarian Faith: The Evangelical Theology of the Ancient Catholic Church*. Edinburgh: T. & T. Clark, 1988.

Tsirpanlis, Constantine N. *The Anthropology of Saint John of Damascus*. Athens: n.p., 1980.

Twombly, Charles C. "The Nature of Christ's Humanity: A Study in Athanasius." *Patristic and Byzantine Review* 8 (1989) 227–41.

Voelker, Walther. *Maximus Confessor als Meister des Geistlichen Lebens*. Wiesbaden: Steiner GMBH, 1965.

Wainwright, A. W. *The Trinity in the New Testament*. London: SPCK, 1962.

Weil, Simone. *Intimations of Christianity Among the Greeks*. 1957. Reprint, London: Ark, 1987.

Welch, Claude. *The Trinity in Contemporary Theology*. London: SCM, 1953.

Wiles, Maurice. *The Making of Christian Doctrine: A Study in the Principles of Early Doctrinal Development*. Cambridge: Cambridge University Press, 1967.

———. *The Spiritual Gospel: The Interpretation of the Fourth Gospel in the Early Church*. Cambridge: Cambridge University Press, 1960.

Wiles, Maurice, and Mark Santer, eds. *Documents in Early Christian Thought*. Cambridge: Cambridge University Press, 1975.

Williams, Charles. *The Descent of the Dove: A Short History of the Holy Spirit in the Church*. 1939. Reprint, Grand Rapids: Eerdmans, 1980.

Williams, Rowan. *Arius: Heresy and Tradition*. Grand Rapids: Eerdmans, 2002.

———. *Christian Spirituality*. Atlanta: John Knox, 1980.

Wolfson, H. A. *The Philosophy of the Church Fathers*. Cambridge, MA: Harvard University Press, 1956.

Yannaras, Christos. "The Distinction between Essence and Energies and Its Importance for Theology." *St. Vladimir's Theological Quarterly* 19 (1975) 234–42.

Zizioulas, John D. *Being as Communion: Studies in Personhood and the Church*. Crestwood, NY: St. Vladimir's Seminary Press, 1985.

———. *Communion and Otherness*. Edited by Paul McPartlan. London: T. & T. Clark, 2006.

———. "Human Capacity and Human Incapacity: A Theological Exploration into Personhood." *Scottish Journal of Theology* 28 (1975) 401–48.

www.ingramcontent.com/pod-product-compliance
Lightning Source LLC
Chambersburg PA
CBHW071451160426
43195CB00013B/2080